ISBN: 9781314521108

Published by:
HardPress Publishing
8345 NW 66TH ST #2561
MIAMI FL 33166-2626

Email: info@hardpress.net
Web: http://www.hardpress.net

THE

THEORY OF POLITICAL ECONOMY.

a

THE

THEORY OF POLITICAL ECONOMY.

BY

W. STANLEY JEVONS, M.A. (Lond.)

PROFESSOR OF LOGIC AND POLITICAL ECONOMY
IN OWENS COLLEGE, MANCHESTER.

London and New York

MACMILLAN AND CO.

1871.

OXFORD:

BY T. COMBE, M.A., E. B. GARDNER, AND E. PICKARD HALL,

PRINTERS TO THE UNIVERSITY.

PREFACE.

THE contents of the following pages can hardly meet with ready acceptance among those who regard the Science of Political Economy as having already acquired a nearly perfect form. I believe it is generally supposed that Adam Smith laid the foundations of this science ; that Malthus, Anderson, and Senior added important doctrines; that Ricardo systematised the whole; and, finally, that Mr. J. S. Mill filled in the details and completely expounded this branch of knowledge. Mr. Mill appears to have had a similar notion ; for he distinctly asserts that there was nothing in the Laws of Value which remained for himself or any future writer to clear up. Doubtless it is difficult to help feeling that opinions adopted and confirmed by such eminent men have much weight of probability in their favour. ·Yet, in the other sciences this weight of authority has not been allowed to restrict the free examination of new opinions and theories; and it has often been ultimately proved that authority was on the wrong side.

There are· many portions of Economical doctrine which appear to me as scientific in form as they are consonant with facts. I would especially mention the Theories of Population and Rent, the latter a theory of a distinctly mathematical character which seems to give a clue to the correct mode of treating the whole science. Had Mr. Mill contented himself with asserting the unquestionable truth of the Laws of Supply and Demand, I should have agreed with him. As founded upon facts, those laws cannot be shaken by any theory;

but it does not therefore follow, that our conception of Value is perfect and final. Other generally accepted doctrines have always appeared to me purely delusive, especially the so-called Wage Fund Theory. This theory pretends to give a solution of the main problem of the science—to determine the wages of labour; yet, on close examination, its conclusion is found to be a mere truism, namely, that the average rate of wages is found by dividing the whole amount appropriated to the payment of wages by the number of those between whom it is divided. Some other supposed conclusions of the science are of a less harmless character, as, for instance, those regarding the advantage of exchange (see p. 134).

In this work I have attempted to treat Economy as a Calculus of Pleasure and Pain, and have sketched out, almost irrespective of previous opinions, the form which the science, as it seems to me, must ultimately take. I have long thought that as it deals throughout with quantities, it must be a mathematical science in matter if not in language. I have endeavoured to arrive at accurate quantitative notions concerning Utility, Value, Labour, Capital, &c., and I have often been surprised to find how clearly some of the most difficult notions, especially that most puzzling of notions *Value*, admit of mathematical analysis and expression. The Theory of Economy thus treated presents a close analogy to the science of Statical Mechanics, and the Laws of Exchange are found to resemble the Laws of Equilibrium of a lever as determined by the principle of virtual velocities. The nature of Wealth and Value is explained by the consideration of indefinitely small amounts of pleasure and pain, just as the Theory of Statics is made to rest upon the equality of indefinitely small amounts of energy. But I believe that dynamical branches of the Science of Economy may remain to be developed, on the consideration of which I have not at all entered.

Mathematical readers may perhaps think that I have explained some elementary notions, that of the Degree of Utility, for instance, with unnecessary prolixity. But it is to the neglect of Economists to obtain clear and accurate notions of quantity and degree of utility that I venture to attribute the present difficulties and imperfections of the science ; and I have purposely dwelt upon the point at full length. Other readers will perhaps think that the occasional introduction of mathematical symbols obscures instead of illustrating the subject. But I must request all readers to remember that, as Mathematicians and Political Economists have hitherto been two nearly distinct classes of persons, there is no slight difficulty in preparing a mathematical work on Economy with which both classes of readers may not have some grounds of complaint.

It is very likely that I have fallen into errors of more or less importance, which I shall be glad to have pointed out ; and I may say that the cardinal difficulty of the whole theory is alluded to in the section of Chapter IV upon the ' Ratio of Exchange,' beginning at p. 91. So able a mathematician as my friend Professor Barker, of Owens College, has had the kindness to examine some of the proof sheets carefully ; but he is not, therefore, to be held responsible for the correctness of any part of the work.

My enumeration of the previous attempts to apply mathematical language to Political Economy does not pretend to completeness even as regards English writers ; and I find that I forgot to mention a remarkable pamphlet ' On Currency ' published anonymously in 1840 (London, Charles Knight and Co.) in which a mathematical analysis of the operations of the Money Market is attempted. The method of treatment is not unlike that adopted by Dr. Whewell, to whose Memoirs a reference is made; but finite or occasionally infinitesimal differences are introduced. On the success of this anonymous theory I have not formed an opinion; but the subject is one which must some day be solved by mathematical analysis. Garnier, in his treatise on Political Economy, mentions several continental mathematicians who have written on the subject of Political Economy; but I have not been able to discover even the titles of their Memoirs.

CONTENTS.

CHAPTER I.

INTRODUCTION.

CHAPTER II.

THEORY OF PLEASURE AND PAIN.

Contents.

CHAPTER III.

THEORY OF UTILITY.

CHAPTER IV.

THEORY OF EXCHANGE.

CHAPTER V.

THEORY OF LABOUR.

CHAPTER VI.

THEORY OF RENT.

CHAPTER VII.

THEORY OF CAPITAL.

CHAPTER VIII.

CONCLUDING REMARKS.

THE

THEORY OF POLITICAL ECONOMY.

CHAPTER I.

INTRODUCTION.

THE science of Political Economy rests upon a
few notions of an apparently simple character.
Utility, value, labour, land, capital, are the
elements of the subject; and whoever has a
thorough comprehension of their nature, must
possess or be soon able to acquire a knowledge
of the whole science. As almost every economical writer has remarked, it is in the simple
elements that we require the most care and
precision, since the least error of conception
must vitiate all our deductions. Accordingly, I
have devoted the following pages to a complete
investigation of the conditions and relations of
the above-named notions.

B

Repeated reflection and inquiry have led me to the somewhat novel opinion, that *value depends entirely upon utility*. Prevailing opinions make labour rather than utility the origin of value; and there are even those who distinctly assert, that labour is the *cause of value*. I show, on the contrary, that we have only to trace out carefully the natural laws of the variation of utility, as depending upon the quantity of commodity in our possession, in order to arrive at a satisfactory theory of exchange, of which the ordinary laws of supply and demand are a necessary consequence. This theory is in perfect harmony with facts; and whenever there is any apparent reason for the belief, that labour is the cause of value, we obtain a complete explanation of the reason. Labour is found often to determine value, but only in an indirect manner, by varying the degree of utility of the commodity through an increase in the supply.

These views are not put forward in a hasty or ill-considered manner. All the chief points of the theory were sketched out ten years ago; but they were then published only in the form of a very brief paper communicated to the Statistical or Economic Section of the British

Association at the Cambridge Meeting in the year 1862. A still briefer abstract of that paper was inserted in the Report of the Meeting [a], and the paper itself was not printed until June 1866 [b]. Since writing that paper, I have, over and over again, questioned the truth of my own notions, but without ever finding any reason to doubt their substantial correctness. I have therefore thought it needless to delay any longer submitting the theory to the criticism of those who are interested in the progress of Political Economy.

Mathematical Character of the Science.

It seems perfectly clear that Economy, if it is to be a science at all, must be a mathematical science. There exists much prejudice against attempts to introduce the methods and language of mathematics into any branch of the moral sciences. Most persons appear to hold that the physical sciences form the proper sphere of mathematical method, and that the moral sciences demand some other method, I know not what. My theory of Economy, however, is

[a] 'Report of the British Association, Cambridge, 1862.' 'Reports of Sections,' p. 158.

[b] 'Journal of the Statistical Society,' vol. xxix. p. 282.

purely mathematical in character. Nay, finding that the quantities with which we have to deal are subject to continuous variation, I do not hesitate to use the appropriate branch of mathematical science, involving though it does the fearless consideration of infinitely small quantities. The theory consists in applying the differential calculus to the familiar notions of wealth, utility, value, demand, supply, capital, interest, labour, and all the other notions belonging to the daily operations of industry. As the complete theory of almost every other science involves the use of that calculus, so we cannot have a true theory of Political Economy without its aid.

To me it seems that our science must be mathematical, simply because it deals with quantities. Wherever the things treated are capable of being *more or less* in magnitude, there the laws and relations must be mathematical in nature. The ordinary laws of supply and demand treat entirely of quantities of commodity demanded or supplied, and express the mode in which the quantities vary in connection with the price. By this fact the laws are mathematical : Economists cannot deprive them of their nature by denying them the name ; they might as well try to alter red light by calling it blue. Whether or not the mathematical laws of Economy are stated in words, or in the usual symbols, x, y, z, is an accident, or a mere matter of convenience. The most complicated mathematical problems may be stated in ordinary language, and their solution might be traced out by words. In fact, some of the most distinguished mathematicians have displayed a great liking for getting rid of their symbols, and expressing their arguments and results in language as nearly as possible approximating to that in common use. Laplace attempted to express the truths of physical astronomy in common language in his admirable 'Système du Monde ;' and Thomson and Tait interweave their great 'Treatise on Natural Philosophy' with an interpretation in ordinary words, supposed to be within the comprehension of general readers.

These attempts, however distinguished and ingenious their authors, soon disclose the inherent defects of the grammar and dictionary for expressing complicated relations. The symbols of mathematical books are not different in nature from language ; they are merely a perfected system of language, adapted to the notions and relations which we need to express. They do not make the mode of reasoning they embody ; they merely facilitate its exhibition and comprehension.   If, then, in Political Economy we have to deal with quantities and complicated relations of quantities, we must reason mathematically ; we do not render the science less mathematical by avoiding the symbols of algebra,—we merely refuse to employ, in a very imperfect science, much needing every kind of assistance, that apparatus of signs which is found indispensable in other sciences.

Prevailing Confusion between Mathematical and Exact Sciences.

Many persons indeed seem to entertain a prejudice against mathematical language, arising out of a confusion between a mathematical science and an exact science.   They think that we must not pretend to calculate unless we have the precise data, which will give a precise answer to our calculations ; but, in reality, there is no such thing as an exact science, except in a comparative sense.   Astronomy is more exact than other sciences, because the position of a planet or a star admits of close

measurement; but, if we examine the methods
of physical astronomy, we find that they are
all approximate. Every solution involves hypo-
theses which are not really true: as, for instance,
that the earth is a smooth, homogeneous sphe-
roid. Even the apparently simpler problems in
statics or dynamics are only hypothetical ap-
proximations to the truth.

We can calculate the effect of a crow-bar,
provided it be perfectly inflexible and have a
perfectly hard fulcrum, which is never the
case [c]. The data are almost wholly deficient
for the complete solution of any one problem
in natural science. Had physicists waited until
their data were perfectly precise before they
brought in the aid of mathematics, we should
have still been in the age of science which
terminated at the time of Galileo.

When we examine the less precise physical
sciences, we find that physicists are, of all men,
most bold in developing their mathematical
theories in advance of their data. Let any one
who doubts this examine Airy's 'Theory of
the Tides [d];' he will find a wonderfully complex

[c] Thomson and Tait's 'Treatise on Natural Philosophy,'
vol. i. p. 337.
[d] 'Encyclopædia Metropolitana.'

mathematical theory which is confessed by its author to be incapable of exact or even approximate application, because the results of the various and often unknown shapes of the seas do not admit of numerical verification. In this and many other cases we may have perfect mathematical theory without the data requisite for precise calculations.

The greater or less accuracy attainable in a mathematical science is a matter of accident, and does not affect the fundamental character of the science. There can be but two classes of sciences—those which are *simply logical,* and *those which, besides being logical, are also mathematical.* If there be any science which determines merely whether a thing be or be not—whether an event will happen, or will not happen—it must be a purely logical science; but if the thing may be greater or less, or the event may happen sooner or later, nearer or farther, then quantitative notions enter, and the science must be mathematical in nature, by whatever name we call it.

Capability of Exact Measurement.

Many will object, no doubt, that the notions which we treat in this science are incapable of any measurement. We cannot weigh, or gauge, or test the feelings of the mind; there is no unit of labour, or suffering, or enjoyment. It might thus seem as if a mathematical theory of Political Economy would be necessarily deprived for ever of any numerical data.

In the first place, I would remark, that nothing is less warrantable in science than an uninquiring and unhoping spirit. In matters of this kind, those who despair are almost invariably those who have never tried to succeed. A man might be allowed to despair had he spent a lifetime on a difficult task without a gleam of encouragement; but the popular opinions on the extension of mathematical theory tend to deter any man from attempting tasks which, however difficult, ought, some day, to be achieved.

If we trace the history of other sciences, we gather no lessons of discouragement. In the case of almost everything which is now exactly measured, we can go back to the time when the vaguest notions prevailed. Previous to the time of Pascal, who would have thought of measuring *doubt* and *belief*? Who could have conceived that the investigation of petty games of chance would have led to the creation of perhaps the most sublime and perfect branch of mathematical science — the theory of probabilities? There are sciences which, even within the memory of men now living, have become exactly quantitative. When Adam Smith founded Political Economy in England, electricity was a vague phenomenon, which was known, indeed, to be capable of more or less, but was not measured nor calculated: it is within the last thirty or forty years that a mathematical theory of electricity, founded on exact data, has been established. We now enjoy the most precise quantitative notions concerning heat, and can measure the temperature of a body to less than $\frac{1}{5000}$ part of a degree Centigrade. Compare this precision with that of the earliest makers of thermometers, the Academicians del Cimento, who used to graduate their instruments by placing them in the sun's rays to obtain a point of fixed temperature.

The late Mr. De Morgan excellently said [e], 'As to some magnitudes, the clear idea of measurement comes soon: in the case of length, for example. But let us take a more difficult one, and trace the steps by which we acquire and fix the idea: say *weight*. What weight is, we

[e] 'Formal Logic,' p. 175.

need not know . . . . . . We know it as a magnitude before we give it a name : any child can
discover the *more* that there is in a bullet, and
the less that there is in a cork of twice its size.
Had it not been for the simple contrivance of
the balance, which we are well assured (how,
it matters not here) enables us to poise equal
weights against one another, that is, to detect
equality and inequality, and thence to ascertain
how many times the greater contains the less,
we might not to this day have had much clearer
ideas on the subject of weight, as a magnitude,
than we have on those of talent, prudence, or
self-denial, looked at in the same light. All
who are ever so little of geometers will remember the time when their notions of an angle, as
a magnitude, were as vague as, perhaps more
so than, those of a moral quality ; and they will
also remember the steps by which this vague-
ness became clearness and precision.'

Now there can be no doubt whatever that
pleasure, pain, labour, utility, value, wealth,
money, capital, &c. are all notions admitting of
quantity : nay, the whole of our actions in industry and trade certainly depend upon comparing quantities of advantage or disadvantage.—Even the most abstract theories of morals

have fully recognised the quantitative character of the subject. Bentham's 'Introduction to the Principles of Morals and Legislation' is thoroughly mathematical in the character of the method. He tells us to estimate the tendency of an action[f] thus: 'Sum up all the values of all the pleasures on the one side, and those of all the pains on the other. The balance, if it be on the side of pleasure, will give the good tendency of the act, upon the whole, with respect to the interests of that individual person; if on the side of pain, the bad tendency of it upon the whole.'

I confess that it seems to me difficult even to imagine how such estimations and summations can be made with any approach to accuracy. Greatly though I admire the clear and precise notions of Bentham, I know not where his numerical data are to be found.

'Then where,' the reader will perhaps ask, 'are your numerical data for estimating pleasures and pains in Political Economy?' I answer, that my numerical data are more abundant and precise than those possessed by any other science, but that we have not yet known how to employ them. The very abundance of

[f] p. 52.

our data is perplexing. There is not a clerk or book-keeper in the country who is not engaged in recording numerical data. The private account books, the great ledgers of merchants and bankers and public offices, the share lists, price lists, bank returns, monetary intelligence, Custom-house and other Government returns, are all full of the kind of numerical data required to render Political Economy an exact mathematical science. Thousands of folio volumes of statistical, parliamentary, or other publications await the labour of the investigator. It is partly the very extent and complexity of the information which deters us from its proper use. But it is chiefly a want of method and completeness in this vast mass of information which prevents our readily employing it in the investigation of the natural laws of Political Economy.

Far be it from me to say that we ever shall have the means of measuring directly the feelings of the human heart. A unit of pleasure or of pain is difficult even to conceive; but it is the amount of these feelings which is continually prompting us to buying and selling, borrowing and lending, labouring and resting, producing and consuming; and it is from the quantitative effects of the feelings that we must estimate their comparative amounts. We can no more know or measure gravity in its own nature than we can measure a feeling, but just as we measure gravity by its effects in the motion of a pendulum, so we may estimate the equality or inequality of feelings by the varying decisions of the human mind. The will is our pendulum, and its oscillations are minutely registered in all the price lists of the markets. I know not when we shall have a perfect system of statistics, but the want of it is the only insuperable obstacle in the way of making Political Economy an exact science. In the absence of complete statistics, the science will not be less mathematical, though it will be infinitely less useful than if, comparatively speaking, exact. A correct theory is the first step towards improvement, by showing what we need and what we might accomplish.

Previous Attempts to employ Mathematical Language in the Moral Sciences.

Several writers have, from time to time, applied the language and processes of mathematical reasoning to the moral or political sciences.

As long ago as the early part of last century, Francis Hutcheson, in his 'Inquiry into the Original of our Ideas of Beauty and Virtue,' gave formulæ for representing the motives of the human mind g. It may be said, perhaps, that little advantage arises from their use, because the relations expressed have not a degree of complexity demanding the aid of symbols. But I have never been able to see anything absurd in their employment, though Hutcheson's example has found few followers.

Among political economists, Dr. Whewell has made the most elaborate attempt to apply mathematical formulæ to the science. In 1829 and 1831 he read to the Cambridge Philosophical Society two long memoirs h, containing a mathematical exposition of the doctrines laid down in Ricardo's 'Principles of Political Economy.' These papers have received the least possible attention from economists; I do not, in fact, remember a single reference to them. Yet

g Third edition, 1729, pp. 186–191.

h 'Mathematical Exposition of some Doctrines of Political Economy.' Cambridge Philosophical Transactions, vol. iii. p. 191. (Read March 1829.)

'Mathematical Exposition of the leading Doctrines in Mr. Ricardo's " Principles of Political Economy and Taxation." ' *Ib.* vol. iv. p. 155. (Read April and May 1831.)

they possess considerable interest, and are remarkable for clearness of style.

These memoirs fail, however, to lead to any satisfactory results, probably because they are a mere translation in symbols of Ricardo's propositions, some of which are of doubtful soundness. The very use of a mathematical language should be to render deductive reasoning easy and sure, so that we can independently reach and prove the conclusions of economists whenever they are true. But this is the reverse of Dr. Whewell's method. I consider, too, that his mathematical processes are wholly unsuited to the science. He treats quantities of demand, supply, wages, profits, interest, &c. as simple discontinuous amounts, and proposes to determine them by equations of a simple kind. He regards questions in economy as little more difficult than sums in arithmetic.

Dr. Whewell's example was followed by Mr. Tozer in memoirs on the effect of machinery upon the wealth of a country and the rate of wages, and on the effect of the non-residence of landlords [i]. These memoirs seem to be almost as able as those of Dr. Whewell, but are of a

[i] 'Mathematical Investigation of the Effect of Machinery on the Wealth of a Country, and the Fund for the Payment of

very similar character ; and it can hardly be said that they lead to new truths. In more recent years, Mr. McLeod has applied algebraic formulæ to economical questions, especially to Banking [k]. I may also mention Professor Fleeming Jenkin's 'Graphic illustrations of the Laws of Supply and Demand,' in an essay published a year or two since [l].

There exists a work by Dr. Lardner [m] on 'Railway Economy,' a statistical treatise on the cost and financial conditions of railway communication, which treats certain questions of Political Economy in a highly scientific and mathematical spirit. Thus the relation of the rate of fares to the gross receipts and net profits of a railway company is beautifully demonstrated in pp. 286–293, by means of a diagram. It is proved that the maximum profit occurs at the point where the curve of gross receipts becomes parallel to the curve of expenses of

Wages.' By John Tozer, B.A. Cambridge Philosophical Transactions, vol. vi. p. 507.

'On the Effect of the Non-residence of Landlords on the Wealth of a Community,' *ib.* vol. vii. p. 189.

[k] 'The Theory and Practice of Banking,' vol. i. p. 189.

'Dictionary of Political Economy,' article *Credit*, &c.

[l] 'Recess Studies.'

[m] 'Railway Economy,' by Dionysius Lardner, D.C.L. London, 1850.

conveyance.   The most advantageous rate of charge in this and many other similar cases is that at which a very small change of the rate makes no appreciable difference in the net profits.

In a work to which I shall have occasion to refer more than once, Mr. Jennings has pointed out that prices, rates of interest, and other distinct money quantities form the *metallic indices*, and the means of observation in our science[n], ' not less capable of being made subservient to the processes of exact calculation than are the instruments of any purely physical art.'   And he adds the remark, ' The results of these principles, when observed, may thus be expressed in figures ; as may also be the anticipated results of their future operation, or such relations as those of quantity and value, value and rate of production, may be exhibited in the formulæ, and analysed by the different methods of algebra and of fluxions.'   This is a clear statement of the views which I have also adopted.

Of the Measurement of Feeling and Motives.

Many readers may, even after reading the preceding remarks, consider it quite impos-

n ' Natural Elements of Political Economy,' pp. 259, 260.

sible to create such a calculus as is here contemplated, because we have no means of defining and measuring quantities of feeling, like we can measure a mile, or a right angle, or any other physical quantity. I have granted that we can hardly form the conception of a unit of pleasure or pain, so that the numerical expression of quantities of feeling seems to be out of the question. But we only employ units of measurement in other things to facilitate the comparison of quantities; and if we can compare the quantities directly, we do not need the units. Now the mind of an individual is the balance which makes its own comparisons, and is the final judge of quantities of feeling. As Mr. Bain says[o], 'It is only an identical proposition to affirm that the greatest of two pleasures, or what appears such, sways the resulting action; for it is this resulting action that alone determines which is the greater.'

Pleasures, in short, are, for the time being, as the mind estimates them; so that we cannot make a choice, or manifest the will in any way, without indicating thereby an excess of pleasure in some direction. It is true that the mind often hesitates and is perplexed in

[o] 'The Emotions and the Will,' p. 447.

making a choice of great importance : this indicates either varying estimates of the motives concerned, or a feeling of incapacity to grasp the quantities concerned. I should not for a moment think of claiming for the mind any accurate power of measuring and adding and subtracting feelings, so as to get an exact balance. We can seldom or never affirm that one pleasure is a multiple of another in quantity; but the reader who carefully criticises the following theory will find that it seldom involves the comparison of quantities of feeling differing much in amount. The theory turns upon those critical points where pleasures are nearly, if not quite, equal. I never attempt to estimate the whole pleasure gained by purchasing a commodity; the theory merely expresses that, when a man has purchased enough, he derives equal pleasure from the possession of a small quantity more or from the money price of it. Similarly, the whole amount of pleasure that a man gains by a day's labour hardly enters the question; it is when a man is doubtful whether to increase his hours of labour or not, that we discover an equality between the pain of that extension and the pleasure of the increase of possessions derived from it.

The reader will find, again, that there is never, in a single instance, an attempt made to compare the amount of feeling in one mind with that in another. I see no means by which such comparison can ever be accomplished. The susceptibility of one mind may, for what we know, be a thousand times greater than that of another. But, provided that the susceptibility was different in a like ratio in all directions, we should never be able to discover the profoundest difference. Every mind is thus inscrutable to every other mind, and no common denominator of feeling is possible. Even if we could compare the feelings of different minds, we should not need to do so; for one mind only affects another indirectly. Every event in the outward world is represented in the mind by a corresponding motive, and it is by the balance of these that the will is swayed.

I must here point out that, though the theory presumes to investigate the condition of a mind, and bases upon this investigation the whole of Political Economy, practically it is an aggregate of individuals which will be treated. The general form of the laws of Economy is the same in the case of individuals and nations; and, in reality, it is a law operating in the case of multitudes of individuals which gives rise to the aggregate represented in the transactions of a nation.   Practically, however, it is quite impossible to detect the operation of general laws of this kind in the actions of one or a few individuals.   The motives and conditions are so numerous and complicated, that the resulting actions have the appearance of caprice, and are beyond the analysis and prediction of science. With every increase in the price of such a commodity as sugar, we ought, theoretically speaking, to find every person reducing his consumption by a small amount, and according to some regular law. In reality, many persons would make no change at all; a few, probably, would go to the extent of dispensing with the use of sugar altogether while its cost was excessive. It is by examining the average consumption of sugar in a large population that we should detect a continuous variation connected with the variation of price by a constant law. It will not, of necessity, happen, that the law will be exactly the same in the case of aggregates and individuals, unless all those individuals be of the same character and position as regards wealth and habits; but there will be a more or less regular law to which the same kind of formulæ will apply. The use of an average, or, what is the same, an aggregate result depends upon the high probability that accidental and disturbing causes will operate, in the long run, as often in one direction as the other, so as to neutralise each other. Provided that we have a sufficient number of independent cases, we may then detect the effect of any *tendency*, however slight. Accordingly, questions which appear, and perhaps are quite, indeterminate as regards individuals, may be capable of exact investigation and solution in regard to great masses and wide averages.

Logical Method of Political Economy.

I may add a few words on the logical character of the science of Political Economy, as to which somewhat diverse opinions have been held. I think that Mr. Mill is right in considering it an instance of the Concrete Deductive Method, or, as I have elsewhere proposed to call it, the Complete Method p, which Mr. Mill has so admirably described q. Political Economy is, undoubtedly, grounded upon observed facts, and is, so far, an inductive science ; but it does

---

p ' Elementary Lessons in Logic,' p. 258.
q ' System of Logic,' book vi. chap. 9, s. 1.

not proceed by an elaborate collection of facts and their gradual classification, as Mr. Richard Jones would have us believe. A few of the simplest principles or axioms concerning the nature of the human mind must be taken as its first starting-point, just as the vast theories of mechanical science are founded upon a few simple laws of motion. That every person will choose the greater apparent good ; that human wants are more or less quickly satiated ; that prolonged labour becomes more and more painful, are a few of the simple inductions on which we can ground, as I attempt to show, a complete deductive mathematical theory. Thence we deduce the laws of supply and demand, the nature and laws of that ambiguous and difficult conception, value ; especially the laws governing its relation to labour or cost of production. The theory, however, needs verification, and this it finds in the agreement of its conclusions with common sense and direct observation.

The theory may, perhaps, be described as the mechanics of human interest. I may have committed oversights in explaining its details ; but I conceive that, in its main features, this theory, whether useful or useless, must be the true one. Its method is as sure and demonstrative as that of kinematics or statics, nay, almost as self-evident, when the real meaning of the formulæ is fully seized, as are the elements of Euclid.

The usefulness of the theory is a different question from that of its truth, and is one upon which I am not quite so confident. To attain correct and clear notions of the nature of value and capital is, indeed, the first essential of a knowledge of Political Economy; and to this object the following pages are in a great degree devoted. But I do not hesitate to say, too, that Political Economy might be gradually erected into an exact science, if only commercial statistics were far more complete and accurate than they are at present, so that the formulæ could be endowed with exact meaning by the aid of numerical data. These data would consist chiefly in accurate accounts of the quantities of goods possessed and consumed by the community, and the prices at which they are exchanged. There is no reason whatever why we should not have those statistics, except the cost and trouble of collecting them, and the unwillingness of persons to afford information. The quantities themselves to be measured and registered are most concrete and precise. In a few cases we already have information approximating to completeness, as when a commodity like tea, sugar, coffee, or tobacco is wholly imported. But when articles are untaxed, and more or less produced within the country, we have yet the vaguest notions of the quantities consumed. Some slight success is now, at last, attending the efforts to gather agricultural statistics; and the great need felt by men engaged in the cotton and other trades to obtain accurate accounts of stocks, imports, and consumption, will probably lead to the publication of far more accurate information than we have hitherto enjoyed.

The deductive science of Economy must be verified and rendered useful by the purely inductive science of Statistics. Theory must be invested with the reality and life of fact. But the difficulties of this union are immensely great, and I appreciate them quite as much as does Professor Cairnes in his admirable lectures ' On the Character and Logical Method of Political Economy.' I make hardly any attempt to employ statistics in this work, and thus I do not pretend to any numerical precision. But, before we attempt any investigation of facts, we must have correct theoretical notions; and of what are here presented, I would say, in the words of Hume, in his 'Essay on Commerce,' 'If false, let them be rejected : but no one has a right to entertain a prejudice against them merely because they are out of the common road.'

Relation of Political Economy to Moral Philosophy.

I wish to say a few words, in this place, upon the relation of Economy to moral science. The theory which follows is entirely based on a calculus of pleasure and pain ; and the object of Economy is to maximise happiness by purchasing pleasure, as it were, at the lowest cost of pain. The language employed may be open to misapprehension, and it may seem as if pleasures and pains of a gross kind were treated as the all-sufficient motives to guide the mind of man. I have no hesitation in accepting the Utilitarian theory of morals which does uphold the effect upon the happiness of mankind as the criterion of what is right and wrong. But I have never felt that there is anything in that theory to prevent our putting the widest and highest interpretation upon the terms used.

Jeremy Bentham put forward the Utilitarian theory in the most uncompromising manner. According to him, whatever is of interest or importance to us must be the cause of pleasure or of pain; and when the terms are used with a sufficiently wide meaning, pleasure and pain include all the forces which drive us to action. They are explicitly or implicitly the object of all our calculations, and form the ultimate quantities to be treated in all the moral sciences. The words of Bentham on this subject may require some explanation and qualification, but they are too grand and too full of truth to be omitted. 'Nature,' he says[r], 'has placed mankind under the governance of two sovereign masters—*pain* and *pleasure.* It is for them alone to point out what we ought to do, as well as to determine what we shall do. On the one hand the standard of right and wrong, on the other the chain of causes and effects, are fastened to their throne. They govern us in all we do, in all we say, in all we think: every effort we can make to throw off our subjection will serve but to demonstrate and confirm it. In words a man

[r] 'An Introduction to the Principles of Morals and Legislation,' by Jeremy Bentham. Edition of 1823, vol. i. p. 1.

may pretend to abjure their empire; but, in reality, he will remain subject to it all the while. The *principle_of_utility-* recognises this subjection, and assumes it for the foundation of that system, the object of which is to rear the fabric of felicity by the hands of reason and of law. Systems which attempt to question it, deal in sounds instead of sense, in caprice instead of reason, in darkness instead of light.'

In connection with this passage we may take that of Paley, who says, with his usual clear brevity[s], 'I hold that pleasures differ in nothing but in continuance and intensity.'

The acceptance or non-acceptance of the basis of the Utilitarian doctrine depends, in my mind, on the exact interpretation of the language used.

As it seems to me, the feelings of which a man is capable are of various grades. He is always subject to mere physical pleasure or pain, necessarily arising from his bodily wants and susceptibilities. He is capable also of mental and moral feelings of several degrees of elevation. A higher motive may rightly overbalance all considerations belonging even to the next

[s] 'Principles of Moral and Political Philosophy,' book i. chap. 6.

lower range of feelings; but so long as the
higher motive does not intervene, it is surely
both desirable and right that the lower motives
should be balanced against each other.   Starting with the lowest stage—it is, a man's duty,
as it is his natural inclination, to earn sufficient
food and whatever else may best satisfy his
proper and moderate desires   If the claims of a
family or of friends fall upon him, it may become
desirable that he should deny his own desires
and even his physical needs their customary
gratification.   But the claims of a family are
only a step to a higher grade of duties.

The safety of a nation, the welfare of great
populations, may happen to depend upon his
exertions, if he be a soldier or a statesman :
claims of a very strong kind may now be over-
balanced by claims of a still stronger kind.   Nor
should I venture to say that, at any point, we
have reached the highest rank—the supreme motives which should guide the mind. The statesman may discover a conflict between motives;
a measure may promise, as it would seem, the
greatest good to great numbers, and yet there
may be motives of uprightness and honour—that
may hinder or forbid his promoting the measure.   How such difficult questions may be

rightly determined it is not my purpose to inquire here.

The Utilitarian theory holds, that all forces influencing the mind of man are pleasures and pains; and Paley went so far as to say, that all pleasures and pains are of one kind only. Mr. Bain has carried out this view to its complete extent, saying [t], 'No amount of complication is ever able to disguise the general fact, that our voluntary activity is moved by only two great classes of stimulants; either a pleasure or a pain, present or remote, must lurk in every situation that drives us into action.' The question certainly appears to turn upon the language used. Call any motive which attracts to a certain action pleasure, and that which deters pain, and it becomes impossible to deny that all actions are prompted by pleasure or by pain. But it then becomes indispensable to admit that a single higher pleasure will entirely neutralise a vast extent and continuance of lower pains. It seems hardly possible to admit Paley's statement, except with an interpretation that would probably reverse his intended meaning. Motives and feelings are certainly of the same kind to the extent that we

[t] 'The Emotions and the Will,' p. 460.

are able to weigh them against each other; but they are, nevertheless, almost incomparable in power and authority.

My present purpose is accomplished in pointing out this hierarchy of feeling, and assigning a proper place to the pleasures and pains with which Economy deals. It is the lowest rank of feelings which we here treat. The calculus of utility aims at supplying the ordinary wants of man at the least cost of labour. Each labourer, in the absence of other motives, is supposed to devote his energy to the accumulation of wealth. A higher calculus of moral right and wrong would be needed to show how he may best employ that wealth for the good of others as well as himself. But when that higher calculus gives no prohibition, we need the lower calculus to gain us the utmost good in matters of moral indifference. There is no rule of morals to forbid our making two blades of grass grow instead of one, if, by the wise expenditure of labour, we can do so. And we may certainly say, with Bacon, 'while philosophers are disputing whether virtue or pleasure be the proper aim of life, do you provide yourself with the instruments of either.'

CHAPTER II.

THEORY OF PLEASURE AND PAIN.

Of Pleasure and Pain as Quantities.

PROCEEDING to consider how pleasure and pain can be estimated as magnitudes, we must undoubtedly accept what Bentham has laid down upon this subject. 'To a person,' he says [a], ' considered *by himself*, the value of a pleasure or pain, considered *by itself*, will be greater or less according to the four following circumstances :—

    (1) Its *intensity*.

    (2) Its *duration*.

    (3) Its *certainty* or *uncertainty*.

    (4) Its *propinquity* or *remoteness*.

These are the circumstances which are to be considered in estimating a pleasure or a pain considered each of them by itself.'

[a] Introduction, p. 49.

D

Bentham [b], indeed, goes on to consider three other circumstances which relate to the ultimate and complete effect of any act or feeling; these . are—

(5) *Fecundity*, or the chance a feeling has of being followed by feelings of. the same kind: that is, pleasures, if it be a pleasure; pains, if it be a pain.

(6) *Purity*, or the chance it · has of not being followed by feelings of an opposite kind.   And

(7) *Extent*, or the number of persons to whom it extends, and who are affected by it.

These three last circumstances are of the highest importance as regards the theory of morals; but they will not enter into the more simple and restricted problem which we attempt to solve in Political Economy.

A feeling, whether of pleasure or of pain, may be regarded as having essentially two dimensions.   Every feeling must last some time, and it may last a longer or shorter time : while it lasts, it may be more or less acute and intense.   If, in two instances, the duration of feeling is the same, that will possess the greater magnitude which is the most intense; or we may say that, with the same duration, the magnitude will be proportional to the intensity when properly expressed.   On the other hand, if the intensity of a feeling were to remain constant, the magnitude of the feeling would increase with its duration.   Two days of the same degree of happiness are to be twice as much desired as one day; two days of suffering are to be twice as much feared.   If the intensity ever remained fixed, the whole magnitude would be found by multiplying the number of units of intensity into the number of units of duration.   Pleasure and pain, then, are magnitudes possessing two dimensions, just as an area or superficies possesses the two dimensions of length and breadth.

In almost every case, however, the intensity of a feeling will change from moment to moment.   Incessant variation characterises our feelings, and this is the source of the main difficulties of the subject.   Nevertheless, if these variations can at all be traced out, or any approach to method and law detected, it will not be impossible to form a conception of the resulting quantity of feeling.   We may imagine that the intensity changes at the end of every minute, but remains constant in the intervals. The quantity during each minute will be represented, as in Fig. I, by a rectangle whose narrow base is supposed to correspond to the duration of a minute, and whose height is proportional

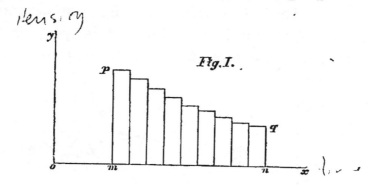

Fig.I.

to the intensity.   Along the line *ox* we measure *time*, and along a parallel to the perpendicular line *oy* we measure *intensity*.   Each of the rectangles between *pm* and *qn* represents the feeling of one minute, or of any other small portion of time assumed.   The aggregate quantity of feeling generated during the time *mn* will then be represented by the aggregate area of the rectangles between *pm* and *qn*.   In this case the intensity of the feeling is supposed to be gradually declining.

But it is an artificial assumption that the intensity would vary by sudden steps and regular intervals. The error thus committed will not be great if the intervals of time are very short, and will be less the shorter the intervals are made. To avoid all error, we may imagine the intervals of time infinitely short; that is, we must treat the intensity as constantly and continuously varying. Thus the proper representation of the variation of feeling is found in

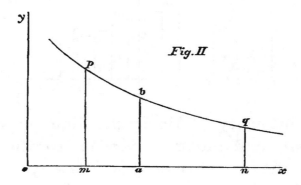

a curve of more or less simple character. In Fig. II the height of each point of the curve *pq*, above the horizontal line *ox*, indicates the intensity of feeling in an indivisible moment of time; and the whole quantity of feeling generated in the time *mn* is measured by the area of the curve between the lines *pm*, *qn*, *mn*, and *pq*. The feeling belonging to any other time, *ma*, will be measured by the space *mabp*, cut off by the perpendicular line *ab*.

Pleasure and Pain related as Positive and Negative Quantities.

It will be readily conceded by the reader that pain is the opposite of pleasure; so that to decrease pain is to increase pleasure; to add pain is to decrease pleasure. Thus we may treat pleasure and pain as positive and negative quantities are treated in algebra. The algebraic sum of a series of pleasures and pains will be obtained by adding the pleasures together and the pains together, and then striking the balance by subtracting the smaller amount from the greater. Our object will always be to maximise the resulting sum in the direction of pleasure, which we may fairly call the positive direction. This we shall really do by accepting everything, and undertaking every action of which the resulting pleasure exceeds the pain which is undergone; we must avoid every object or action which leaves a balance in the other direction.

One of the most important points of the theory will turn upon the exact equality of the pleasure derived from the possession of an

object, and the pain encountered in its acquisition. I am glad, therefore, to quote the following passage from Mr. Bain's treatise on 'The
Emotions and the Will' (p. 30), in which he exactly expresses the opposition of pleasure and
pain :—' When pain is followed by pleasure,
there is a tendency in the one, more or less,
to neutralise the other. When the pleasure
exactly assuages the pain, we say that the two
are equivalent, or equal in amount, although of
opposite nature, like hot and cold, positive and
negative ; and when two different kinds of pleasure have the power of satiating the same
amount of pain, there is fair ground for pro-
nouncing them of equal emotional power. Just
as acids are pronounced equivalent when in
amount sufficient to neutralise the same portion of alkali, and as heat is estimated by the
quantity of snow melted by it, so pleasures are
fairly compared as to their total efficacy on
the mind, by the amount of pain that they are
capable of submerging. In this sense there may
be an effective estimate of degree.'

Of anticipated Feelings.

Bentham has stated [c], that one of the main elements in estimating the force of a pleasure or pain is its *propinquity or remoteness*. It is certain that a very large part of what we experience in life depends not on the actual circumstances of the moment, so much as on the anticipation of future events. As Mr. Bain says [d], 'The foretaste of pleasure is pleasure begun : every actual delight casts before it a corresponding ideal.' Every one must have felt that the enjoyment actually experienced at any moment is but limited in amount, and usually fails to answer to the great anticipations which have been formed. 'Man never is but always to be blest' is a correct description of our ordinary state of mind ; and there is little doubt that, in minds of much intelligence and foresight, the greatest force of feeling and motive is what arises from the anticipation of the future.

Now, between the actual amount of feeling anticipated and that which is felt there must be some natural relation, very variable no doubt,

---

[c] See above, p. 33.
[d] 'The Emotions and the Will,' p. 74.

according to circumstances, according to the intellectual standing of the race, or the character of the individual; and yet subject to some general law of variation. The intensity of present feeling must, to use a mathematical expression, be *some function of the future feeling*, and it must increase as we approach the moment of realisation. The change, again, must be less rapid the further we are from the moment, and more rapid as we come nearer to it. An event which is to happen a year hence affects us on the average about as much one day as another; but an event of importance, which is to take place three days hence, will probably affect us on each of the intervening days more acutely than the last.

This power of anticipation must have a large influence in Economy; for upon it is based all accumulation of stocks of commodity to be consumed at a future time. That class or race of men who have the most foresight will work most for the future. The untutored savage is wholly occupied with the troubles of the moment; the morrow is dimly felt; the limit of his horizon is but a few days off. The wants of a future year, or of a lifetime, are wholly unforeseen. But, in a state of civilisation, a vague though powerful <u>feeling of the future is the main incentive to industry and saving.</u> The cares of the moment are but ripples on the tide of achievement and hope. We may safely call that man happy who, however lowly his position and limited his possessions, can always hope for more than he has, and feel that every moment of exertion tends to realise his aspirations. He, on the contrary, who seizes the enjoyment of the passing moment without regard to coming times, must feel, sooner or later, that his stock of pleasure is on the wane, and that even hope begins to fail.

Uncertainty of Future Events.

In admitting the force of anticipated feeling, we are compelled to take account of the uncertainty of all future events. We ought never to estimate the value of that which may or may not happen as if it would certainly happen. When it is as likely as not that I shall receive £100, the chance is worth but £50, because if, for a great many times in succession, I purchased the chance at this rate, I should almost certainly not lose nor gain. The test of a correct estimation of probabilities is that, in the long run, the calculations prove true on the average. If we apply this rule to all future interests, we must reduce our estimate of any feeling in the ratio of the numbers expressing the probability of its occurrence. If the probability is only one-tenth that I shall have a certain day of pleasure, I ought to anticipate it with one-tenth of the force which would belong to it if certain. In selecting a course of action which depends on uncertain events, as, in fact, does everything in life, I should multiply the force of every future event by the fraction denoting its probability. A great casualty, which is very unlikely to happen, may not be so important as a slight casualty which is nearly sure to happen. Almost unconsciously we make calculations of this kind more or less accurately in all the ordinary judgments of life; and in systems of life, fire, marine, or other insurance, we carry out the calculations to great perfection. In all industry directed to future purposes, we must take similar account of our want of knowledge of what is to be.

CHAPTER III. ·

THEORY OF UTILITY.

Definition of Terms.

PLEASURE and pain are undoubtedly the ulti-mate objects of the Calculus of Economy. To satisfy our wants to the utmost with the least effort—to procure the greatest amount of what is desirable at the expense of the least that is undesirable—in other words, to maximise com-fort and pleasure, is the problem of Economy. But it is convenient to transfer our attention as soon as possible to the physical objects or actions which are the source to us of pleasures or pains. A very large part of the labour of any community is spent upon the production of the ordinary necessaries and conveniences of life, food, clothing, buildings, utensils, furniture, ornaments, &c.; and the aggregate of these ob-jects constitute, therefore, the immediate object of our attention.

It will be convenient at once to introduce and define some terms which will facilitate the expression of the Principles of Economy. By a *commodity* we shall understand any object, or, it may be, any action or service, which can afford pleasure or ward off pain. The name was originally abstract, and denoted the quality of anything by which it was capable of serving man. Having acquired, by a common process of confusion, a concrete signification, it will be well to retain it entirely for that signification, and employ the word *utility* to denote the abstract quality whereby an object serves our purposes, and becomes entitled to rank as a commodity. Whatever can produce pleasure or prevent pain may possess utility. M. Say has correctly and briefly defined utility as 'la faculté qu'ont les choses de pouvoir servir à l'homme, de quelque manière que ce soit.' The food which prevents the pangs of hunger, the clothes which fend off the cold of winter, possess incontestable utility; but we must beware of restricting the meaning of the word by any moral considerations. Anything which an individual is found to desire and to labour for must be assumed to possess for him utility. In the science of Economy we treat men not as they ought to be, but as they are.   Bentham, in establishing the foundation of Moral Science in his great ' Introduction to the Principles of Morals and Legislation' (p. 3), thus comprehensively defines the term in question :—'By utility is meant that property in any object, whereby it tends to produce benefit, advantage, pleasure, good, or happiness (all this, in the present case, comes to the same thing), or (what comes again to the same thing) to prevent the happening of mischief, pain, evil, or unhappiness to the party whose interest is considered.'

This perfectly expresses the meaning of the word in Economy, provided that the will or inclination of the person concerned is taken as the sole criterion, for the time, of what is good and desirable, or painful and evil.

Laws of Human Want the Basis of Economy.

Political Economy must be founded upon a full and accurate investigation of the conditions of utility; and, to understand this element, we must necessarily examine the character of the wants and desires of man.   We, first of all, need a theory of the consumption of wealth.   Mr. J. S. Mill, indeed, has given an opinion inconsistent with this. 'Political Economy,' he says [e], 'has nothing to do with the consumption of wealth, further than as the consideration of it is inseparable from that of production, or from that of distribution. We know not of any laws of the consumption of wealth, as the subject of a distinct science; they can be no other than the laws of human enjoyment.'

But it is surely obvious that Political Economy does rest upon the laws of human enjoyment; and that, if those laws are developed by no other science, they must be developed by economists. We labour to produce with the sole object of consuming, and the kinds and amounts of goods produced must be governed entirely by our requirements. Every manufacturer knows and feels how closely he must anticipate the tastes and needs of his customers: his whole success depends upon it; and, in like manner, the whole theory of Economy depends upon a correct theory of consumption. Many economists have had a clear perception of this truth. Lord Lauderdale distinctly states [f], that

[e] 'Essays on some unsettled Questions of Political Economy,' p. 132.

[f] 'Inquiry into the Nature and Origin of Public Wealth,' second edition, 1819, p. 306.

'the great and important step towards ascertaining the causes of the direction which industry takes in nations . . . . seems to be the
discovery of what dictates the proportion of
demand for the various articles which are produced.' Mr. Senior, in his admirable treatise,
has also recognised this truth, and pointed out
what he calls the *Law of Variety* in human requirements. The necessaries of life are so few
and simple, that a man is soon satisfied in regard to these, and desires to extend his range
of enjoyment. His first object is to vary his
food; but there soon arises the desire of variety
and elegance in dress; and to this succeeds the
desire to build, to ornament, and to furnish—
tastes which are absolutely insatiable where
they exist, and seem to increase with every
improvement in civilisation g.

Bastiat has also observed that human wants
are the ultimate object of Economy; and in his
'Harmonies of Political Economy' he says h,
'*Wants, Efforts, Satisfaction*—this is the circle
of Political Economy.'

g 'Encyclopædia Metropolitana,' art. *Political Economy,*
p. 133. Fifth edition of Reprint, p. 11.

h 'Harmonies of Political Economy,' translated by P. J.
Stirling, 1860, p. 65.

In still later years, M. Courcelle-Seneuil actually commenced his treatise with a definition of *want*—'Le besoin économique est un désir qui a pour but la possession et la jouissance d'un objet matériel[i].' And I conceive that he has given the best possible statement of the problem of Economy when he expresses its object as 'à satisfaire nos besoins avec la moindre somme de travail possible[k].'

Professor Hearn also commences his excellent treatise, entitled 'Plutology, or the Theory of Efforts to supply Human Wants,' with a chapter in which he considers the nature of the wants impelling man to exertion.

The writer, however, who seems to me to have reached the deepest comprehension of the foundation of Economy, is Mr. T. E. Banfield. His course of Lectures delivered in the University of Cambridge in 1844, and published under the title of 'The Organization of Labour,' is highly interesting, but perhaps not always correct. In the following passage[l] he profoundly points out that the scientific basis of Economy

i 'Traité Théorique et Pratique d'Economie Politique,' par J. G. Courcelle-Seneuil, 2me ed. Paris, 1867, tom. i. p. 25.

k *Ib.* p. 33.

l Second edition, p. 11.

E

is in a theory of consumption : I need make no
excuses for quoting this passage at full length.

'The lower wants man experiences in common with brutes. The cravings of hunger and
thirst, the effects of heat and cold, of drought
and damp, he feels with more acuteness than
the rest of the animal world. His sufferings
are doubtless sharpened by the consciousness
that he has no right to be subject to such in-
flictions. Experience, however, shows that privations of various kinds affect men differently
in degree, according to the circumstances in
which they are placed. For some men the privation of certain enjoyments is intolerable, whose
loss is not even felt by others. Some, again, sacrifice all that others hold dear for the gratification
of longings and aspirations that are incompre-
hensible to their neighbours. Upon this complex
foundation of low wants and high aspirations
the Political Economist has to build the theory
of production and consumption.

'An examination of the nature and intensity
of man's wants shows that this connection between them gives to Political Economy its scientific basis. The first proposition of the theory
of consumption is, that *the satisfaction of every
lower want in the scale creates a desire of a higher*

character.⌉ If the higher desire existed previous to the satisfaction of the primary want, it becomes more intense when the latter is removed. The removal of a primary want commonly awakens the sense of more than one secondary privation: thus a full supply of ordinary food not only excites to delicacy in eating, but awakens attention to clothing. The highest grade in the scale of wants, that of pleasure derived from the beauties of nature and art, is usually confined to men who are exempted from all the lower privations. Thus the demand for, and the consumption of, objects of refined enjoyment has its lever in the facility with which the primary wants are satisfied. This, therefore, is the key to the true theory of value. Without relative values in the objects to the acquirement of which we direct our power, there would be no foundation for Political Economy as a science.'

Utility not an Intrinsic Quality.

My principal work now lies in tracing out the exact nature and conditions of utility. It seems strange indeed that economists have not bestowed more minute attention on a subject which doubtless furnishes the true key to the problem of Economy.

In the first place, utility, though a quality of things, is no inherent quality. It might be more accurately described, perhaps, as *a circumstance of things* arising out of their relation to man's requirements. / As Mr. Senior most accurately. says, ' Utility denotes no intrinsic quality in the things which we call useful / it merely expresses their relations to the pains and pleasures of mankind/ We can never, therefore, say absolutely that some objects have utility and others have not./ The ore lying in the mine, the diamond escaping the eye of the searcher, the wheat lying unreaped, the fruit ungathered for want of consumers, have not utility at all. The most - wholesome and necessary kinds of food are useless unless there are hands to collect and mouths to eat them. / Nor, when we consider the matter closely, can we say that all portions of the same commodity possess equal utility./ Water, for instance, may be roughly described as the most useful of all substances. A quart of water per day has the high utility of saving a person from dying in a most distressing manner. Several gallons a day may possess much utility for such purposes as cooking and washing ; but after an adequate supply is secured for these uses, any additional quantity is a matter of indifference. All that we can say, then, is, that water, up to a certain quantity, is indispensable; that further quantities will have various degrees of utility; but that beyond a certain point the utility appears to cease.)

(Exactly the same considerations apply more or less clearly to every other article. A pound of bread per day supplied to a person saves him from starvation, and has the highest conceivable utility. A second pound per day has also no slight utility: it keeps him in a state of comparative plenty, though it be not altogether indispensable. A third pound would begin to be superfluous. It is clear, then, that *utility is not proportional to commodity*: the very same articles vary in utility according as we already possess more or less of the same article. The like may be said of other things. One suit of clothes per annum is necessary, a second convenient, a third desirable, a fourth not unacceptable; but we, sooner or later, reach a point at which further supplies are not desired with any perceptible force, unless it be for subsequent use.

Law of the Variation of Utility.

Let us now investigate this subject a little more closely. (Utility must be considered as measured by, or even as actually identical with, the addition made to a person's happiness.) It is a convenient name for the aggregate of the favourable balance of feeling produced—the sum of the pleasure created and the pain prevented. We must now carefully discriminate between the *total utility* belonging to any commodity and the utility belonging to any particular portion of it. Thus the total utility of the food we eat consists in maintaining life, and may be considered as infinitely great; but if we were to subtract a tenth part from what we eat daily, our loss would be but slight. It might be doubtful whether we should suffer any harm at all. Let us imagine the whole quantity of food which a person consumes on an average during twenty-four hours to be divided into ten equal parts. If his food be reduced by the last part, he will suffer but little; if a second tenth part be deficient, he will feel the want distinctly; the subtraction of the third tenth part will be decidedly injurious; with every subsequent subtraction of a tenth part his sufferings will be more and more serious, until at length he will be upon the verge of starvation. Now, if we call each of the tenth parts *an increment,* the meaning of these facts is, that each increment of food is less necessary, or possesses less utility, than the previous one. To represent this vari- ation of utility, we may make use of space- representations, which I have found it conve- nient to employ in illustrating the laws of Economy in my lectures during seven or eight years past.

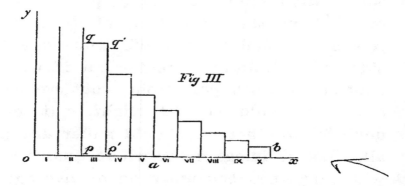

· Let the line *ox* be used as a measure of the quantity of food, and let it be divided into ten equal parts to correspond to the ten parts of food mentioned above. Upon these equal lines are constructed rectangles, and the area of each rectangle may be assumed to represent the util- ity of the increment of food corresponding to its base. Thus the utility of the last increment is small, being proportional to the small rect- angle on x. As we approach towards *o*, each in- crement bears a larger rectangle, that standing upon III being the largest complete rectangle. The utility of the next increment, II, as also that of I, is undefined, since these portions of food would be indispensable to life, and their utility, therefore, infinitely great.

We can now form a clear notion of the utility of the whole food, or of any part of it; for we have only to add together the proper rectangles. The utility of the first half of the food will be the sum of the rectangles standing on the line *oa*; that of the second half will be represented by the sum of the smaller rectangles between *a* and *b*. The total utility of the food will be the whole sum of the rectangles, and will be infinitely great.

The comparative degree of utility of the several portions is, however, the most important point to be considered. (Utility is *a quantity of at least two dimensions*, one dimension consisting in the quantity of the commodity, and another in the intensity of the effect produced upon the consumer.) Now, the quantity of the commodity is measured on the horizontal line *ox*, and the intensity of utility will be measured by the length of the upright lines, or *ordinates*, as they are commonly called by mathematicians. The intensity of utility of the

third increment is measured either by pq, or
$p'q'$, and its utility is the product of the units
in pp' by those in pq.

But the division of the food into ten equal
parts is an arbitrary supposition. If we had
taken twenty or a hundred or more equal
parts, the same general principle would hold
true, namely, that [each small portion would be
less useful and necessary than the last.] The law
may be considered to hold true theoretically,
however small the increments are made; and
in this way we shall at last reach a figure which
is undistinguishable from a continuous curve.
The notion of infinitely small quantities of food
may seem absurd as regards one individual; but,
when we come to consider the consumption of
nations as a whole, the consumption may well
be conceived to increase or diminish by quantities which are, practically speaking, infinitely
small compared with the whole consumption.

The law of the variation of the degree of
utility of food may thus be represented by a
continuous curve pbq (Fig. IV), and the perpendicular height of each point of the curve
above the line ox, represents the degree of
utility of the commodity when a certain amount
has been consumed.

Thus, when the quantity *oa* has been consumed, the degree of utility corresponds to the
length of the line *ab*; for if we take a very

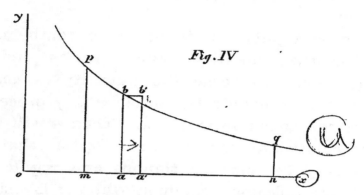

Fig. IV

little more food, *aa'*, its utility will be the product of *aa'* and *ab* very nearly, and more
nearly the less is the magnitude of *aa'*. The
degree of utility is thus properly measured by
the height of a very narrow rectangle corresponding to a very small quantity of food, which
theoretically ought to be infinitely small.

Distinction between Total Utility and Degree of Utility.

We are now in a position fully to appreciate
the difference between the *total utility* of any
commodity and *the degree of utility* of the commodity at any point. These are, in fact, quantities of altogether different kinds, the first being

represented by an area, and the second by a
line. We must consider how we may express
these notions in appropriate mathematical language.

Let x signify, as is usual in mathematical
books, the quantity which varies independently,—in this case the quantity of commodity. Let u denote the *whole utility* proceeding
from the consumption of x. Then u will be, as
mathematicians say, *a function of x;* that is, it
will vary in some continuous and regular, but
probably unknown, manner, when x is made to
vary. Our great object, however, is to express
the *degree of utility.*

By prefixing the sign $\triangle$ to a quantity, mathematicians denote that a very small part of that
quantity is taken into consideration. Thus $\triangle x$
means a very small part of x, the quantity of
commodity; and $x + \triangle x$ therefore means a very
little more commodity than x. Now the utility
of $x + \triangle x$ will be more than that of x as a
general rule. Let the whole utility of $x + \triangle x$ be
denoted by $u + \triangle u$; then it is obvious that the
increment of utility $\triangle u$ belongs to the increment of commodity $\triangle x$; and if, for a moment,
we suppose the degree of utility uniform over
the whole of $\triangle x$, which is nearly true owing to

its smallness, we shall find the corresponding degree of utility by dividing $\triangle u$ by $\triangle x$.

We find these considerations fully illustrated by Fig. IV, in which $oa = x$ and ab will be the degree of utility at the point a. Now, if we increase x by the small quantity aa', or $\triangle x$, the utility may be considered as increased by a small rectangle $abb'a'$, or $\triangle u$; and, since a rectangle is the product of its sides, we find that the line ab, the degree of utility, is represented by the fraction $\dfrac{\triangle u}{\triangle x}$.

The utility of a commodity may, however, be considered to vary with perfect continuity, so that we commit a small error in assuming it to be uniform over the whole increment $\triangle x$. To avoid this we must imagine $\triangle x$ to be reduced to an infinitely small size, $\triangle u$ decreasing with it. The smaller the quantities are the more nearly we shall have a correct expression for ab, the degree of utility at the point a. Thus the *limit* of this fraction $\dfrac{\triangle u}{\triangle x}$, or, as it is commonly expressed, $\dfrac{du}{dx}$, is the degree of utility corresponding to the quantity of commodity x. *The degree of utility is*, in mathematical language, *the differential coefficient of u considered as a function of x*, and will itself be another function of *x*.

We shall seldom need to consider the degree of utility except as regards the last increment which is consumed, and I shall therefore commonly use the expression *final degree of utility* meaning the degree of utility of the last addition, or the next possible addition of a very small, or infinitely small, quantity to the existing stock. In ordinary circumstances, too, the final degree of utility will not be great compared with what it might be. Only in famine or other extreme circumstances do we approach the higher degrees of utility. Accordingly, we can often treat the lower portions of the curve of variation (*pbq*, Fig. IV) which concern ordinary commercial transactions, while we leave out of sight the portions beyond *p* or *q*. It is also evident that we may know the degree of utility at any point while ignorant of the total utility, that is, the area of the whole curve.

The Final Degree of Utility and the Law of its Variation.

The final degree of utility is that function upon which the whole Theory of Economy will

be found to turn.   Political Economists, generally speaking, have failed to discriminate between this function and the total utility.   From
this confusion has arisen much perplexity.   Many
of those commodities which are the most useful
to us are esteemed and desired the least.   We
cannot live a day without water, and yet in
ordinary circumstances we set no value on it.
Why is this?   Simply because we usually have
so much of it that its final degree of utility is
reduced nearly to zero.   We enjoy, every day,
the almost infinite utility of water, but then we
do not need to consume more than we have.
Let the supply run short by drought, and we
begin to feel the higher degree of utility, of
which we think but little at other times.)

The variation of the function expressing the
final degree of utility is the all-important point
in all economical problems.   We may state, as
a general law, that (it varies with the quantity
of commodity, and ultimately decreases as that
quantity increases.)   No commodity can be named
which we continue to desire with the same
force, whatever be the quantity already in use
or possession.   All our appetites are capable of
satisfaction or *satiety* sooner or later, both these
words meaning, etymologically, that we have

had *enough*, so that more is of no use to us. (It does not follow, indeed, that the degree of utility will always sink to zero. This may be the case with many things, especially the simple animal requirements, food, water, air, &c.) But the more refined and intellectual our needs become, the less are they capable of satiety. To the desire for articles of taste, science, or curiosity, when once excited, there is hardly a limit.)

This great principle of the ultimate decrease of the final degree of utility of any commodity is implied in the writings of many economists, though seldom distinctly stated. It is the real law which lies at the basis of Senior's so-called 'Law of Variety.' Indeed, Senior states the law itself. He says: 'It is obvious that our desires do not aim so much at quantity as at diversity. Not only are there limits to the pleasure which commodities of any given class can afford, but the pleasure diminishes in a rapidly increasing ratio long before those limits are reached. Two articles of the same kind will seldom afford twice the pleasure of one, and still less will ten give five times the pleasure of two. In proportion, therefore, as any article is abundant, the number of those who are provided with it, and do not wish, or wish but little, to increase their provision, is likely to be great; and, so far as they are concerned, the additional supply loses all, or nearly all, its utility. And, in proportion to its scarcity, the number of those who are in want of it, and the degree in which they want it, are likely to be increased; and its utility, or, in other words, the pleasure which the possession of a given quantity of it will afford, increases proportionally[m].'

Banfield's 'Law of the Subordination of Wants' also rests upon the same basis. [It cannot be said, with accuracy, that the satisfaction of a lower want *creates* a higher want; it merely permits the higher want to manifest itself.] We distribute our labour and possessions in such a way as to satisfy the more pressing wants first. If food runs short, the all-absorbing question is, how to obtain more, because, at the moment, more pleasure or pain depends upon food than upon any other commodity. But, when food is moderately abundant, its final degree of utility falls very low, and wants of a much more complex and less satiable nature become comparatively prominent.

The writer, however, who appears to me to

m ' Encyclopædia Metropolitana,' p. 133.   Reprint, p. 12.

have most clearly appreciated the nature and importance of the law of utility, is Mr. Richard Jennings, who, in 1855, published a small book called 'The Natural Elements of Political Economy'[n]. This work treats of the physical groundwork of Economy, showing its dependence on physiological laws. It appears to me to display a great insight into the real basis of Economy; yet I am not aware that economists have bestowed the slightest attention on Mr. Jennings' views[o]. I take the liberty, therefore, of giving a full extract from his remarks on the nature of utility. It will thus be seen that the law, as I state it, is no novelty, and that it is only careful deduction from principles in our possession that is needed to give us a correct Theory of Economy.

'To turn from the relative effect of commodities, in producing sensations, to those which are absolute, or dependent only on the quantity of each commodity, it is but too well known to every condition of men, that the degree of each sensation which is produced, is by no means

[n] London : Longmans.
[o] Professor Cairnes is, however, an exception. See his 'Lectures on the Character and Logical Method of Political Economy.' London, 1857, p. 81.

commensurate with the quantity of the commodity applied to the senses . . . . . . These effects require to be closely observed, because they are the foundation of the changes of money price, which valuable objects command in times of varied scarcity and abundance; we shall therefore direct our attention to them for the purpose of ascertaining the nature of the law according to which the sensations that attend on consumption vary in degree with changes in the quantity of the commodity consumed.

' We may gaze upon an object until we can no longer discern it, listen until we can no longer hear, smell until the sense of odour is exhausted, taste until the object becomes nauseous, and touch until it becomes painful; we may consume food until we are fully satisfied, and use stimulants until more would cause pain. On the other hand, the same object offered to the special senses for a moderate duration of time, and the same food or stimulants consumed when we are exhausted or weary, may convey much gratification. If the whole quantity of the commodity consumed during the interval of these two states of sensation, the state of satiety and the state of inanition, be conceived to be divided into a number of equal parts, each marked with its proper degrees of sensation, the question to be determined will be, what relation does the difference in the degrees of the sensation bear to the difference in the quantities of the commodity? First, with respect to all commodities, our feelings show that the degrees of satisfaction do not proceed *pari passu* with the quantities consumed; they do not advance equally with each instalment of the commodity offered to the senses, and then suddenly stop; but diminish gradually, until they ultimately disappear, and further instalments can produce no further satisfaction. In this progressive scale the increments of sensation resulting from equal increments of the commodity are obviously less and less at each step,—each degree of sensation is less than the preceding degree. Placing ourselves at that middle point of sensation, the *juste milieu*, the *aurea mediocritas*, the ἄριστον μέτρον of sages, which is the most usual status of the mass of mankind, and which, therefore, is the best position that can be chosen for measuring deviations from the usual amount, we may say that the law which expresses the relation of degrees of sensation to quantities of commodities is of this character: if the average or temperate quantity of commodities be increased, the satisfaction derived is increased in a less degree, and ultimately ceases to be increased at all; if the average or temperate quantity be diminished, the loss of more and more satisfaction will continually ensue, and the detriment thence arising will ultimately become exceedingly great ' P.

Distribution of Commodity in different Uses.

The principles of utility may be illustrated by considering the mode in which we distribute a commodity when it is capable of several uses. There are articles which may be employed for many distinct purposes : thus, barley may be used either to make beer, spirits, bread, or to feed cattle ; sugar may be used to eat, or for producing alcohol ; timber may be used in construction, or as fuel ; iron and other metals may be applied to many different purposes. Imagine, then, a community in the possession of a certain stock of barley ; what principles will regulate their mode of consuming it ? Or, as we have not yet reached the subject of exchange, imagine an isolated family, or even an individual, possessing an adequate stock, and using some in one way and some in another. The theory

P pp. 96–99.

of utility gives, theoretically speaking, a complete solution of the question.

Let s be the whole stock of some commodity, and let it be capable of three distinct uses. Then we may represent the three quantities appropriated to these uses by x_1, y_1, and z_1, it being a necessary condition that $x_1 + y_1 + z_1 = s$. The person may be conceived as successively expending small quantities of the commodity; now it is the inevitable tendency of human nature to choose that course which offers the most apparent good at the moment. Hence, when the person remains satisfied with the distribution he has made, it follows that no alteration would yield him more pleasure; which amounts to saying that an increment of commodity would yield exactly as much utility in one use as in another. Let $\triangle u_1$, $\triangle u_2$, $\triangle u_3$, be the increments of utility arising from consuming one equal increment of commodity in three different ways. When the distribution is completed, we ought to have $\triangle u_1 = \triangle u_2 = \triangle u_3$; or at the limit we have the equations

$$\frac{du_1}{dx} = \frac{du_2}{dy} = \frac{du_3}{dz},$$

which are true when x, y, z, are respectively equal to x_1, y_1, z_1. We must, in other words, have the *final degrees of utility* in the three uses equal.

We might sometimes find these equations fail. Even when x is equal to $\frac{99}{100}$ of the stock, its degree of utility might still exceed the utility attaching to the remaining $\frac{1}{100}$ part in either of the other uses. This would mean that it was preferable to give the whole commodity to the first use. Such a case might perhaps be said to be not the exception but the rule; for, whenever a commodity is capable of only one use, the circumstance is theoretically represented by saying, that the final degree of utility in this employment always exceeds that in any other employment.

Under peculiar circumstances great changes may take place in the consumption of a commodity. In a time of scarcity the utility of barley as food might rise so high as to exceed altogether its utility, even as regards the smallest quantity, in producing alcoholic liquors; its consumption in the latter way would then cease. In a besieged town the employment of articles becomes revolutionised. Things of great utility in other respects are ruthlessly applied to strange purposes. In Paris a vast stock of horses were eaten, not so much because they were useless in other ways, as because they were needed more strongly as food. A certain stock of horses had, indeed, to be retained as a necessary aid to locomotion, so that the equation of the degrees of utility never wholly failed.

Duration of Utility.

As utility corresponds to, and is measured by, pleasure produced, and as pleasure is a quantity of two dimensions, intensity and duration, so utility must be conceived as capable of duration. In a great many cases this is evidently true. Furniture, utensils, buildings, books, gems, ornaments, &c., may last a long time and possess more or less utility all the time. If the degree of utility of any such object be constant, the total amount of utility will be proportional to the duration. But the utility may be more or less independently of the time, so that in such cases utility is clearly a quantity of three dimensions. We have seen (p. 56) that utility has two dimensions depending upon the *quantity* of commodity enjoyed and the final degree of its utility. We must now add a third dimension depending upon the length of time during which the commodity can retain its useful qualities. We have more or less need of a thing; we may be more or less fully supplied with that thing; and can enjoy it a longer or shorter time.

Actual, Prospective, and Potential Utility.

[The difficulties of Political Economy are mainly the difficulties of conceiving clearly and fully the conditions of utility.] Even at the risk of being tiresome, I will therefore more minutely point out how various are the senses in which a thing may be said to have utility.

It is quite usual, and perhaps correct, to call iron or water or timber a useful substance; but we may mean by these words at least three distinct facts. [We may mean that a particular piece of iron is at the present moment actually useful to some person; or that, although not actually useful, it is expected to be useful at a future time; or we may only mean that it would be useful if it were in the possession of some person needing it.] The iron rails of a railway, the iron which composes the Britannia Bridge, or an ocean steamer, is actually useful; the iron lying in a merchant's store is not useful at present, though it is expected soon to be so; but there is a vast quantity of iron existing in the bowels of the earth, which has all the physical properties of iron, and might be useful if extracted, though it never will be. These are instances of *actual, prospective, and potential utility.*

It will be apparent that *potential utility* does not really enter into the science of Political Economy, and when I speak of *utility* simply, I do not mean the term to include potential utility. It is a question of physical science whether a substance possesses qualities which might make it suitable to our needs if it were within our reach. Only when there arises some degree of probability, however slight, that a particular object will be needed, does it acquire *prospective utility* capable of rendering it a desirable possession. But a very large part in industry, and the science of industry, belongs to *prospective utility.* We can at any one moment use only a very small part of what we possess. By far the greater part of what we hold might be allowed to perish at any moment, without harm, if we could have it re-created with equal ease at a future moment, when need of it arises.

We might also distinguish, as is customary with French economists, between *direct* and *indirect utility.* Direct utility attaches to a thing like food which we can actually apply to satisfy our wants. But things which have no direct utility may be the means of procuring us such by exchange, and they may therefore be said to have indirect utility [q]. To the latter form of utility I have elsewhere applied the name *acquired utility* [r]. This distinction is not the same as that which is made in the Theory of Capital between *mediate* and *immediate utility*, the former being that of any implement, machine, or other means of procuring commodities possessing *immediate* and *direct utility*—that is, the power of satisfying want [s].

The most advantageous Distribution of a Commodity from time to time.

We have seen that when a commodity is capable of being used for different purposes, definite principles regulate its application to those purposes. A similar question arises when a stock of commodity is in hand, and must be expended over a certain interval of time more or less definite. The science of Economy must point out the mode of consuming it to the greatest advantage—that is, with a maximum of utility. If we reckon all future pleasures

---

[q] Garnier, 'Traité d'Economie Politique,' 5me ed. p. 11.
[r] See Chapter IV.   [s] See Chapter VII.

and pains as if they were present, the solution will be exactly the same as in the case of different uses. If a commodity has to be distributed over n days' use, and v_1, v_2, &c. be the final degrees of utility on each day's consumption, then we ought clearly to have

$$v_1 = v_2 = v_3 = \ldots = v_n.$$

It may, however, be uncertain during how many days we may require the stock to last. The commodity might be of a perishable nature, so that if we keep some of it for ten days, it might become unserviceable, and its utility be sacrificed. Assuming that we can estimate more or less exactly the probability of its remaining good, let p_1 p_2 p_3 . . . p_{10} be these probabilities. Then, on the principle (p. 42) that a future pleasure or pain must be reduced in proportion to its want of certainty, we have the equations $v_1\,p_1 = v_2\,p_2 = \ldots = v_{10}\,p_{10}.$ The general result is, that as the probability is less, the commodity assigned to each day is less, so that v will be greater.

So far we have taken no account of the varying influence of an event according to its propinquity or remoteness. The distribution of commodity described is that which should be made and would be made by a being of perfect good sense and foresight. To secure a maximum of benefit in life, all future events, all future pleasures or pains, should act upon us with the same force as if they were present, allowance being made for their uncertainty. The factor expressing the effect of remoteness should, in short, always be unity, so that time should have no effect. But no human mind is constituted in this perfect way : a future feeling is always less influential than a present one. To take this fact into account, let q_1, q_2, q_3, &c. be the undetermined fractions which express the ratios of the present pleasures or pains to those future ones from whose anticipation they arise. Having a stock of commodity in hand, our tendency will be to distribute it so that the following equations will hold true—

$$v_1\, p_1\, q_1 = v_2\, p_2\, q_2 = v_3\, p_3\, q_3 = \ldots = v_n p_n q_n.$$

It will be an obvious consequence of these equations that less commodity will be assigned to future days in some proportion to the intervening time.

An interesting problem, involving questions of prospective utility and probability, is found in the case of a vessel at sea, which is insufficiently victualled for the probable length of voyage to the nearest port. The actual length of the voyage depends on the winds, and must be uncertain; but we may suppose that it will almost certainly last ten days or more, but not more than thirty days. It is apparent that if the food were divided into thirty equal parts, partial famine and suffering would be certainly endured for the first ten days, to ward off later evils which may very probably not be encountered. To consume one-tenth part of the food on each of the first ten days would be still worse, as almost certainly entailing starvation on the following days. To determine the most beneficial distribution of the food, we should require to know the probability of each day between the tenth and thirtieth days forming part of the voyage, and also the law of variation of the degree of utility of food. The whole stock ought then to be divided into thirty portions, allotted to each of the thirty days, and of such magnitude that the final degrees-of-utility multiplied by the probabilities are all equal. Thus, let v_1, v_2, v_3, &c. be the final degrees of utility of the first, second, third, and other days supplied, and p_1, p_2, p_3, &c. the probabilities that the days in question will form part of the voyage; then we ought to have

$$p_1\, v_1 = p_2\, v_2 = p_3\, v_3 = \ \cdots \ = p_{29}\, v_{29} = p_{30}\, v_{30}.$$

If these equations did not hold, it would be beneficial to transfer a small portion from one lot to some other lot.   As the voyage is supposed certainly to last the first ten days, we have $p_1 = p_2 = \ldots = p_{10} = 1$;
hence we must have

$$v_1 = v_2 = \ldots = v_{10} ;$$

whence it will follow that the allotments to the first ten days should be equal.   They should afterwards decrease according to some regular law; for, as the probability decreases, the final degree of utility should increase in inverse proportion.

CHAPTER IV.

THEORY OF EXCHANGE.

Importance of Exchange in Economy.

EXCHANGE is so important a process in the maximising of utility and the saving of labour, that some economists have regarded their science as treating of this operation alone. Utility arises from commodities being brought in suitable quantities and at the proper times into the possession of persons needing them; and it is by exchange, more than any other means, that this is effected. Trade is not indeed the only method of Economy: a single individual may gain in utility by a proper consumption of the stock in his possession. The best employment of labour and capital by a single person is also a question disconnected from that of exchange, and which must yet be treated in the science. But, with these exceptions, I am perfectly willing to agree with the high importance attributed to exchange.

It is impossible to have a correct idea of the science of Economy without a perfect comprehension of the Theory of Exchange; and I find it both possible and desirable to consider this subject before introducing any notions concerning labour or the production of commodities. In these words of Mr. Mill I thoroughly concur: 'Almost every speculation respecting the economical interests of a society thus constituted, implies some theory of value: the smallest error on that subject infects with corresponding error all our other conclusions; and anything vague or misty in our conception of it, creates confusion and uncertainty in everything else.'   But when he proceeds to say, 'Happily, there is nothing in the laws of Value which remains for the present or any future writer to clear up; the theory of the subject is complete'[a]—he utters that which it would be rash to say of any of the sciences.

[a] 'Principles of Political Economy,' book iii. chap. i. § i.

*Ambiguity of the term Value, and proposed
introduction of the expression—
Ratio of Exchange.*

I must, in the first place, point out the
thoroughly ambiguous and unscientific character of the term *value*. Adam Smith noticed the
extreme difference of meaning between *value in
use* and *value in exchange*; and it is usual for
the best writers on Economy to caution their
readers against the confusion to which they are
liable. But I do not believe that either writers
or readers can avoid the confusion so long as
they use the word. In spite of the most acute
feeling of the danger, I often detect myself
using the word improperly; nor do I think that
the best authorities in Economy escape the
danger.

Let us turn to Mr. Mill's definition of Value [b],
and we at once see the weakness of the term.
He tells us—'Value is a relative term. The
value of a thing means the quantity of some
other thing, or of things in general, which it exchanges for.' Now, if there is any fact certain
about value, it is, that it means not an object at

[b] 'Principles of Political Economy,' book iii, chap. 6.

G

all, but a quality, attribute, or rather a circumstance of an object. Value implies, in fact, a relation; but if so, it cannot possibly be *some other thing*. A student of Economy has no hope of ever being clear and correct in his ideas of the science if he thinks of value as at all a *thing* or *object*, or even as anything which lies in a thing or object. Persons are thus led to speak of such a nonentity as *intrinsic value*. There are, doubtless, qualities inherent in such a substance as gold or iron which influence its value; but the word Value, so far as it can be correctly used, merely expresses *the circumstance of its exchanging in a certain ratio for some other-substance.* If a ton of pig-iron exchanges in a market for an ounce of standard gold, neither the iron is value, nor the gold; nor is there value in the iron nor in the gold. The notion of value is concerned only in the fact or circumstance of one exchanging for the other. Thus it is scientifically incorrect to say that the value of the ton of iron *is* the ounce of gold : we thus convert value into a concrete thing; and it is, of course, equally incorrect to say that the value of the ounce of gold is the ton of iron. The more correct and safe expression is, that *the value of the ton of iron is equal to the value of the ounce of gold*, or that their values are as one to one.

Value in exchange expresses nothing but a ratio, and the term should not be used in any other sense. To speak simply of the value of an ounce of gold is as absurd as to speak of the *ratio of the number seventeen*. What is the ratio of the number seventeen? The question admits no answer, for there must be another number named in order to make a ratio; and the ratio will differ according to the number suggested. What is the value of iron compared with that of gold?—is an intelligible question. The answer consists in stating the ratio of the quantities exchanged.

In the popular use of the word Value there is inextricable confusion with the notion of utility; and the conclusion to which I shall come, that exchange does depend entirely on degrees of utility, gives some countenance to the confusion. To avoid all difficulty, I shall discontinue the use of the word Value altogether, and substitute the unequivocal expression *Ratio of Exchange.* When we speak of the ratio of exchange of pig-iron and gold, there can be no possible doubt that we mean merely the quantity of one given for the other.

Definitions of Market and Trading Body.

Before proceeding to the Theory of Exchange, it will be desirable to place beyond doubt the meanings of two other terms which I shall frequently employ.

By a *Market* I shall mean much what commercial men use it to express. Originally a market was a public place in a town where provisions and other objects were exposed for sale; but the word has been generalised, so as to mean any body of persons who are in intimate business relations and carry on extensive transactions in any commodity. A great city may contain as many markets as there are important branches of trade, and these markets may or may not be localised. The central point of a market is the public exchange,—mart or auction rooms, where the traders agree to meet and transact business. In London, the Stock Market, the Corn Market, the Coal Market, the Sugar Market, and many others, are distinctly localised; in Manchester, the Cotton Market, the Cotton Waste Market, and others. But this distinction of locality is not necessary. The traders may be spread over a whole town, or region of country, and yet make a market, if they are, by means of fairs, meetings, published price lists, the post office, or otherwise, in close communication with each other. Thus, the common expression *Money Market* denotes no locality: it is applied to the aggregate of those bankers, capitalists, and other traders who lend or borrow money, and who constantly exchange information concerning the course of business.

In Political Economy we may usefully adopt this term with a clear and well-defined meaning. By a market I shall mean two or more persons dealing in two or more commodities, whose stocks of those commodities and intentions of exchanging are known to all. It is also essential that the ratio of exchange between any two persons should be known to all the others. It is only so far as this community of knowledge extends that the market extends. Any persons who are not acquainted at the moment with the prevailing ratio of exchange, and whose stocks are not available for want of communication, must not be considered part of the market. Secret or unknown stocks of a commodity must also be considered beyond reach of a market so long as they remain secret and unknown. Every individual must be considered as exchanging from a pure regard to his own requirements or private interests, and there must be perfectly free competition, so that any one will exchange with any one else upon the slightest advantage appearing. There must be no conspiracies for absorbing and holding supplies to produce unnatural ratios of exchange. Were a conspiracy of farmers to withhold all corn from market, the consumers might be driven, by starvation, to pay prices bearing no proper relation to the existing supplies, and the ordinary conditions of the market would be thus overthrown.

The theoretical conception of a perfect market is more or less completely carried out in practice. It is the work of brokers in any extensive market to organise the exchanges, so that every purchase shall be made with the most thorough acquaintance with the conditions of the trade. Each broker strives to have the best knowledge of the conditions of supply and demand, and the earliest intimation of any change. He is in communication with as many other traders as possible, in order to have the widest range of information, and the greatest chance of making suitable exchanges. It is only thus that a definite market price can be ascertained at every moment, and varied according to the frequent news capable of affecting buyers and sellers. By the mediation of a body of brokers a complete consensus is established, and the stocks of every seller or the demands of every buyer are brought into the market. It is of the very essence of trade to have wide and constant information. A market, then, is theoretically perfect only when all traders have perfect knowledge of the conditions of supply and demand, and the consequent ratio of exchange; and in such a market, as we shall now see, there can only be one ratio of exchange of one uniform commodity at any moment.

So essential is a knowledge of the real state of supply and demand to the smooth procedure of trade and the real good of the community, that I conceive it would be quite legitimate to compel the publication of any requisite statistics. Secrecy can only conduce to the profit of speculators who gain from great fluctuations of prices. Speculation is advantageous to the public only so far as it tends to equalise prices; and it is, therefore, against the public good to allow speculators to foster artificially the inequalities of prices by which they profit. The welfare of millions both of consumers and producers depends upon an accurate knowledge of the stocks of cotton and corn; and it would, therefore, be no unwarrantable interference with the liberty of the subject to require any information as to the stocks in hand. In Billingsgate fish market it has been a regulation that salesmen shall fix up in a conspicuous place every morning a statement of the kind and amount of their stock c; and such a regulation, whenever it could be enforced on other markets, would always be to the advantage of every one except a few traders.

I find it necessary to adopt some expression for any number of people whose aggregate influence in a market, either in the way of supply or demand, we have to consider. By a *trading body* I mean, in the most general manner, any body either of buyers or sellers. The trading body may be a single individual in one case; it may be the whole inhabitants of a continent in another; it may be the individuals of a trade diffused through a country in a third. England and North America will be trading bodies if we are considering the corn we receive from America in exchange for iron and other goods. The continent of Europe is a trading body as

c Waterston's 'Cyclopædia of Commerce,' ed. 1846, p. 466.

purchasing coal from England. The farmers of
England are a trading body when they sell corn
to the millers, and the millers both when they
buy corn from the farmers and sell flour to the
bakers.

I use the expression with this very wide
meaning, because the principles of exchange
are the same in nature, however wide or narrow may be the market considered. Every
trading body is either an individual or an aggregate of individuals, and the law, in the case
of the aggregate, must depend upon the fulfil-
ment of law in the individuals. We cannot
usually observe any precise and continuous variation in the wants and deeds of an individual,
because the action of extraneous motives, or
what would seem to be caprice, overwhelms
minute tendencies. As I have already remarked (p. 22), a single individual does not
vary his consumption of sugar, butter, or eggs
from week to week by infinitesimal amounts,
according to each small change in the price.
He probably continues his ordinary consumption until accident directs his attention to a
rise in price, and he then, perhaps, discontinues
the use of the articles altogether for a time.
But the aggregate, or what is the same, the

average consumption of a large community will be found to vary continuously in a more or less rapid manner. The most minute tendencies make themselves apparent in a wide average. Thus, our laws of Economy will be theoretically true in the case of individuals, and practically true in the case of large aggregates; and the general principles will be the same, whatever the extent of the trading body considered. I am justified, then, in using the expression with the utmost generality.

At the same time, it would be an obvious error to suppose that the particular character of an economical law holding true of a great aggregate will be exactly the same as that of any individual. Only when the individuals are of perfectly uniform character will their average supply or demand for any commodity represent that of an individual. But every community is usually composed of individuals differing widely in powers, wants, habits, and possessions. An average will therefore partly depend upon the comparative numbers belonging to each class.

Of the Ratio of Exchange.

When a commodity · is perfectly uniform or homogeneous in quality, all portions may be indifferently used in place of equal portions: hence, in the same market, and at the same moment, all portions must be exchanged at the same ratio. There can be no reason why a person should treat exactly similar things differently, and the slightest excess in what is demanded for one over the other will cause him to take the latter instead of the former. In nicely-balanced exchanges it is a very minute scruple which will turn the scale and govern the choice. A minute difference of quality in a commodity may thus give rise to preference, and cause the ratio of exchange to differ. But where no difference exists at all, or where no difference is known to exist, there can be no ground for preference whatever. If, in selling a quantity of perfectly equal and uniform barrels of flour, a merchant arbitrarily fixed different prices on them, a purchaser would of course select the cheaper ones; and where there was absolutely no difference in the thing purchased, even a penny in the price might be a valid

ground of choice.   Hence follows what is undoubtedly true, with proper explanations, that
*in the same open market, at any moment, there
cannot be two prices for the same kind of arti*cle.
Such differences as may practically occur arise
from extraneous circumstances, such as the de-
fective credit of the purchasers, their imperfect
knowledge of the market, and so on.

Though the price of the same commodity
must be uniform at any one moment, it may
vary from moment to moment, and must be
conceived as in a state of continual change.
Theoretically speaking, it may not be possible
to buy two portions of the same commodity
successively at the same ratio of exchange, because, no sooner has the first portion been
bought, than the conditions of utility are altered.   When exchanges are made on a large
scale, this result will be verified in practice.   If
a wealthy person invested £100,000 in the funds
in the morning, it is hardly likely that the
operation could be repeated in the afternoon at
the same price.   In any market, if a person
goes on buying largely, he will ultimately raise
the price against himself.   Thus it is apparent
that extensive purchases would best be made
gradually, so as to secure the advantage of a

lower price upon the earlier portions. In theory this effect of exchange upon the ratio of exchange must be conceived to exist in some degree, however small may be the purchases made. Strictly speaking, the ratio of exchange at any moment is that of dy to dx, of an infinitely small quantity of one commodity to the infinitely small quantity of another which is given for it. The ratio of exchange is really a differential coefficient. The quantity of any article purchased is a function of the price with which it is purchased, and the ratio of exchange expresses the rate at which the quantity of the article increases compared with what is given for it.

We must carefully distinguish, at the same time, between the Statics and Dynamics of this subject. The real condition of industry is one of perpetual motion and change. Commodities are continually being manufactured and exchanged and consumed. If we wished to have a complete solution of the problem in all its natural complexity, we should have to treat it as a problem of dynamics. But it would surely be absurd to attempt the more difficult question when the more easy one is yet so imperfectly within our power. It is only as a purely statical problem that I can venture to treat the action of exchange. Holders of commodities will be regarded not as continuously passing on these commodities in streams of trade, but as possessing certain fixed amounts which they exchange until they come to equilibrium.

It is much more easy to determine the point at which a pendulum will come to rest than to calculate the velocity at which it will move when displaced from that point of rest. Just so, it is a far more easy task to lay down the conditions under which trade is completed and interchange ceases, than to attempt to ascertain at what rate trade will go on when equilibrium is not attained.

The difference will present itself in this form: dynamically we could not treat the ratio of exchange otherwise than as the ratio of dy and dx, infinitesimal quantities of commodity; but in the statical view of the question we can substitute the ratio of the finite quantities y and x. Thus, from the self-evident principle, stated on pp. 91–2, that there cannot, in the same market, at the same moment, be two different prices for the same uniform commodity, it follows that *the last increments in an act of exchange must be exchanged in the same ratio as the whole quantities exchanged.* Suppose that two commodities are bartered in the ratio of x for y; then every m^{th} part of x is given for the mth part of y, and it does not matter for which of the mth parts. No part of the commodity can be treated differently to any other. We may carry this division to an indefinite extent by imagining m to be constantly increased, so that, at the limit, even an infinitely small part of x must be exchanged for an infinitely small part of y, in the same ratio as the whole quantities. This result we may express by stating that the increments concerned in the process of exchange must obey the equation

$$\frac{dy}{dx} = \frac{y}{x}.$$

The use which we shall make of this equation will be seen in the next section.

The Theory of Exchange.

The keystone of the whole Theory of Exchange, and of the principal problems in Political Economy, lies in this proposition — *The ratio of exchange of any two commodities will be inversely as the final degrees of utility of the quantities of commodity available for consump-*

tion after the exchange is effected.　When the
reader has reflected a little upon the meaning
of this proposition, he will see, I think, that it
is necessarily true, if the principles of human
nature have been correctly represented in previous pages.

Imagine, for a moment, that there is one
trading body possessing only corn, and another
possessing only beef.　It is certain that, under
these circumstances, a portion of the corn may
be given in exchange for a portion of the beef
with a considerable increase of utility.　How
are we to determine at what point the exchange will cease to be beneficial?　This question must involve both the ratio of exchange
and the degrees of utility.　Suppose, for a
moment, that the ratio of exchange is approximately that of ten pounds of corn for one
pound of beef : then, if to the trading body
which possesses corn, ten pounds of corn are
less useful than one of beef, that body will
desire to carry the exchange further.　Should
the other body possessing beef find one pound
less useful than ten pounds of corn, this body
will also be desirous to continue the exchange.
Exchange will thus go on till each party has
obtained all the benefit that is possible, and

loss of utility would result if more were exchanged. Both parties, then, rest in satisfaction and equilibrium, and the degrees of utility
have come to their level, as it were.

This point of equilibrium will be known by
the criterion, that an infinitely small amount
of commodity exchanged in addition, at the
same rate, will bring neither gain nor loss of
utility. In other words, if increments of commodities be exchanged at the established ratio,
their utilities will be equal for both parties.
Thus, if ten pounds of corn were of exactly
the same utility as one pound of beef, there
would be neither harm nor good in further
exchange at this ratio.

It would be hardly possible to represent this
theory completely in a diagram, but the accompanying figure may, perhaps, render it clearer.

Fig V.

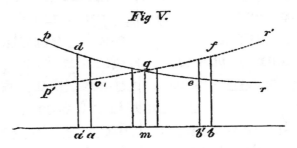

The line *pqr* is a small portion of the curve of
utility of one commodity, while the broken line

H

$p'q\,r'$ is the like curve of another commodity which has been reversed and superposed on the other.   Owing to this reversal, the quantities of the first commodity are measured along the base line from a towards b, whereas those of the second must be measured in the opposite direction.   Let units of both commodities be represented by equal lengths.: then the little line $a'a$ indicates an increase of the first commodity, and a decrease of the second.   Assume the ratio of exchange to be that of unit for unit, or 1 to 1 : then, by receiving the commodity $a'a$ the person will gain the utility $a\,d$, and lose the utility $a'c$; or he will make a net gain of the utility corresponding to the curvilinear figure cd.   He -will, therefore, wish to extend the exchange.   If he were to go up to the point b', and were still proceeding, he would, by the next small exchange, gain the utility $b\,e$, and lose $b'f$; or he woul l have a net loss of ef.   He would, therefore, have gone too far, and it is pretty obvious that the point of intersection, q, defines the place where he would stop with the greatest advantage.   It is there that a net gain is converted into a net loss, or rather where, for an indefinitely small quantity, there is neither gain nor loss.   To represent an indefinitely small quantity, or even an exceedingly small quantity, on a diagram is, of course, impossible; but on either side of the line *mq* I have represented the utilities of a small quantity of commodity more or less, and it is apparent that the net gain or loss upon the exchange of these quantities would be comparatively trifling.

Symbolic Statement of the Theory.

To represent this process of reasoning in symbols, let $\triangle x$ denote a small increment of corn, and $\triangle y$ a small increment of beef exchanged for it. Now our principle of uniformity comes into play. As both the corn and the beef are homogeneous commodities, no parts can be exchanged at a different ratio from other parts in the same market : hence, if x be the whole quantity of corn given for y, the whole quantity of beef received, $\triangle y$ must have the same ratio to $\triangle x$ as y to x; or, we have

$$\frac{\triangle y}{\triangle x} = \frac{y}{x}, \quad \text{or} \quad \triangle y = \frac{y}{x}\triangle x.$$

Now, in a state of equilibrium, the utilities of these increments must be equal in the case of each party, in order that neither more nor less exchange would be desirable : hence the utility per unit of beef must be $\frac{y}{x}$ times that of corn; or, considering the increments as infinitely small, the degrees of utility will be inversely as the magnitudes of the increments.

Let us now suppose that the first body, A, originally possessed the quantity a of corn, and that the second body, B, possessed the quantity b of beef. As the exchange consists in giving x of corn for y of beef, the state of things after exchange will be as follows :—

A holds $a - x$ of corn, and y of beef.

B   „ x of corn, and $b - y$ of beef.

Let $\phi_1(a - x)$ denote the final degree of utility of corn to A, and $\phi_2 x$ the corresponding function for B. Also let $\psi_1 y$ denote A's final degree of utility for beef, and $\psi_2(b - y)$ B's similar function. Then, as explained on pp. 95–98, A will not be satisfied unless the following equation holds true—

$$\phi_1(a - x) \,.\, dx = \psi_1 y \,.\, dy \,;$$

or $$\frac{\phi_1(a - x)}{\psi_1 y} = \frac{dy}{dx}.$$

Hence, substituting for the second member by the equation given on p. 95, we have

$$\frac{\phi_1(a - x)}{\psi_1 y} = \frac{y}{x}.$$

What holds true of A will also hold true of B, *mutatis mutandis.* He must also derive exactly equal utility from the final increments, otherwise it will be for his interest to exchange either more or less; and he will disturb the conditions of exchange. Hence the following equation must hold true—

$$\psi_2 \, (b - y) \, . \, dy = \phi_2 \, x \, . \, dx \, ;$$

or, substituting as before,

$$\frac{\phi_2 \, x}{\psi_2 \, (b - y)} = \frac{y}{x} \, .$$

We arrive, then, at the conclusion, that whenever two commodities are exchanged for each other, and *more or less can be given or received in indefinitely small quantities*, the quantities exchanged satisfy two equations, which may be thus stated in a concise form—

$$\frac{\phi_1 \, (a - \dot{x})}{\psi_1 \, y} = \frac{y}{x} = \frac{\phi_2 \, x}{\psi_2 \, (b - y)} \, .$$

The two equations are sufficient to determine the results of exchange; for there are only two unknown quantities concerned, namely, x and y, the quantities given and received.

A vague notion has existed in the minds of economical writers, that the conditions of exchange may be expressed in the form of an

equation. Thus, Mr. Mill has said [d] : 'The idea
of a *ratio,* as between demand and supply, is
out of place, and has no concern in the matter :
the proper mathematical analogy is that of an
equation. Demand and supply, the quantity
demanded and the quantity supplied, will be
made equal.' Mr. Mill here speaks of an equation as only a proper mathematical *analogy.*
But if Political Economy is to be a real science
at all, it must not deal with analogies ; it must
reason by real equations like all the other
sciences which have reached at all a systhem-
atic character. But, after all, Mr. Mill's equation
is a different one from those at which we have
arrived above ; it consists in stating that the
quantity x given by A is equal to the quantity
x received by B. But this must necessarily be
the case if any exchange takes place at all.
The theory of value, as expounded by Mr. Mill,
fails to reach the root of the matter, and show
how the amount of demand or supply is caused
to vary. And Mr. Mill does not perceive that,
as there must be two parties and two quantities to every exchange, there must be two
equations. Nevertheless, the theory is perfectly
consistent with the laws of supply and demand ;

d 'Principles of Political Economy,' book iii. chap. 2, § 4.

and if we had the functions of utility determined, it would be possible to throw them
into a form clearly expressing the equivalence
of supply and demand.

We may regard x as the quantity demanded
on one side and supplied on the other; similarly, y is the quantity supplied on the one
side and demanded on the other. Now, when
we hold the two equations to be simultaneously
true, we assume that the x and y of one equation equal those of the other.

The laws of supply and demand are thus a
result of what seems to me the true theory
of value or exchange.

Impediments to Exchange.

We have hitherto <u>treated the theory as if the
action of exchange could be carried on without
any trouble or cost. In reality, the cost of conveyance is nearly always of importance</u>, and is
sometimes the principal element in the question. <u>To the cost of mere transport</u> must be
added a variety of charges of brokers, agents,
packers, dock, harbour, light dues, &c., together
with any <u>custom duties</u> imposed either on the
importation or exportation of commodities. All
these charges, whether necessary or arbitrary,

are so many impediments to commerce, and tend to reduce its advantages. The effect of any one such charge, or of the aggregate of the costs of exchange, can be represented in our formulæ in a very simple manner.

In whatever mode the charges are payable, they may be conceived as paid by the surrender on importation of a certain fraction of the commodity received ; for the amount of the charges will almost always be proportional to the quantity of goods, and, if expressed in money, can be considered as turned into commodity.

Thus, if A gives x, this is not the quantity received by B ; a part of x is previously subtracted, so that B receives say mx, which is less than x, and the terms of exchange must be adjusted on his part so as to agree with this condition. Hence the second equation will be

$$\frac{y}{mx} = \frac{\phi_2\,(mx)}{\psi_2(b-y)} \; .$$

Again, A, though giving x, will not receive the whole of y; but say ny, so that his equation similarly is

$$\frac{\phi_1\,(a-x)}{\psi_1\,(ny)} = \frac{ny}{x} \; .$$

The result is, that there is not one ratio of
exchange, but two ratios ; and the more these
differ, the less advantage there will be in exchange. It is obvious that A has either to remain satisfied with less of the second commodity than before, or has to give more of his
own in purchasing it.

The equations of impeded exchange may also
be stated in the concise form—

$$\frac{\phi_1(a-x)}{n \cdot \psi_1(ny)} = \frac{y}{x} = \frac{m \cdot \phi_2(mx)}{\psi_2(b-y)} \, .$$

Illustrations of the Theory of Exchange.

As stated above, the Theory of Exchange may
seem to be of a somewhat abstract and perplexing character; but it is not difficult to find
practical illustrations which will show how it
is verified in the actual working of a great
market. The ordinary laws of supply and demand, when properly stated, are the practical
manifestation of the theory. Considerable dis-
cussion has indeed recently taken place concerning these laws, in consequence of Mr. W. T.
Thornton's writings upon the subject in the
'Fortnightly Review,' and in his work on the
'Claims of Labour.' Mr. Mill, although he had
previously declared the Theory of Value to be

complete and perfect (see p. 80), has been led by Mr. Thornton's arguments to allow that modification is required. For my own part, I think that most of Mr. Thornton's arguments are beside the question. He suggests that there are no regular laws of supply and demand, because he adduces certain cases in which no regular variation can take place. Those cases might be indefinitely multiplied, and yet the laws in question would not be touched. Of course, laws which assume a continuity of variation are inapplicable where continuous variation is impossible. Economists can never be free from difficulties unless they will distinguish between a theory and the *application of a theory*. Because, in retail trade, in English or Dutch auction, or other particular instances, we cannot at once observe the operation of the laws of supply and demand, it is not in the least to be supposed that those laws are false. In fact, Mr. Thornton seems to allow that, if prospective demand and supply are taken into account, they become substantially true. But, in the actual working of any market, the influence of future events would never be neglected either by a merchant or an economist.

Though Mr. Thornton's objections are mostly beside the question, his remarks have served to show that the action of the laws of supply and demand was inadequately explained by previous economists. What constitutes the demand and the supply was not carefully enough investigated. As Mr. Thornton points out, there may be a number of persons willing to buy; but if their highest offer is ever so little short of the lowest price which the seller is willing to take, their influence is *nil*. If in an auction there are ten people willing to buy a horse at £20, but not higher, their demand instantly ceases when any one person offers £21. I am inclined not only to accept such a view, but to carry it much further. Any change in the price of an article will be determined not with regard to the large numbers who might or might not buy it at other prices, but by the few who will or will not buy it according as a change is made close to the existing price.

The theory consists in carrying out this view to the point of asserting, that it is only comparatively insignificant quantities of supply and demand which are at any moment operative on the ratio of exchange. This is practically verified by what takes place in any very

large market — say that of the Consolidated
Funds.   As the whole amount of the funds
is nearly eight hundred millions sterling, the
quantity bought or sold by any ordinary purchaser is almost indefinitely small in comparison.   Even £1,000 worth of stock may be taken
as an infinitesimally small increment, because
it does not appreciably affect the total existing
supply.   Now the theory consists in asserting,
that the market price of the funds is affected
from hour to hour not by the enormous
amounts which *might* be bought or sold at extreme prices, but by the comparatively insignificant amounts which *are* being sold or bought
at the existing prices.   A change of price is
always occasioned by the overbalancing of the
inclinations of those who will or will not sell
just about the point at which prices stand.
When Consols are $93\frac{1}{2}$, and business is in a
tranquil state, it matters not how many buyers
there are at 93, or sellers at 94.   They are
really off the market.   Those only are operative
who may be made to buy or sell by a rise or
fall of an eighth or a sixteenth.   The question
is, whether the price shall remain at $93\frac{1}{2}$, or
rise to $93\frac{9}{16}$, or fall to $93\frac{7}{16}$.   This is determined by the sale or purchase of comparatively

very small amounts. It is the purchasers who find a little stock more useful to them than the corresponding sum of money, who make the price rise by $\frac{1}{16}$. When the price of the funds is very steady and the market quiescent, it means that the stocks are distributed among holders in such a way that the exchange of more or less at the prevailing price is a matter of indifference.

In practice, no market ever long fulfils the theoretical conditions of equilibrium, because, from the various accidents of life and business, there are sure to be many people every day compelled to sell or having sudden strong inducements to buy. There is nearly always, again, the influence of prospective supply or demand depending upon the political intelligence of the moment. But we shall never have a Science of Political Economy unless we learn to discern the operation of law even among the most perplexing accidents and interruptions.

Various Problems in the Theory of Exchange.

We have considered hitherto only one simple case of the Theory of Exchange. In all other cases where the commodities are capable of indefinite subdivision, the principles will be exactly the same, but the particular conditions may be subject to much variation.

We may, firstly, express the conditions of a very great market where vast quantities of some stock are available, so that any one small trader will not appreciably affect the ratio of exchange. This ratio is, then, approximately a fixed number, and each trader exchanges at that ratio just so much as suits him. These circumstances may be represented by supposing A to be a trading body possessing two very large stocks of commodities, a and b. Let C be a person who possesses a comparatively small quantity c of the second commodity, and gives a portion of it, y, which is small compared with b, in exchange for a portion x of a, which is small compared with a. Then, after exchange, we shall find A in possession of the quantities $a-x$ and $b+y$, and C in possession of x and $c-y$. The equations will become

$$\frac{\phi_1 (a-x)}{\psi_1 (b+y)} = \frac{y}{x} = \frac{\phi_2 x}{\psi_2 (c-y)}.$$

Since $a-x$ and $b+y$ do not appreciably differ from a and b, we may substitute the latter quantities, and we have, for the first equation, approximately,

$$\frac{\phi_1 a}{\psi_1 b} = \frac{y}{x} = m.$$

The ratio of exchange being a fixed ratio determined by the conditions of the trading body A, there is, in reality, only one undetermined quantity, x, the quantity of commodity which C finds it advantageous to purchase by expending part of c. This will now be determined by the equation

$$\frac{\phi_1 a}{\psi_1 b} = \frac{\phi_2 x}{\psi_2 (c - mx)}.$$

This equation will represent the condition in regard to any one distinct commodity of a very small country trading with a much larger one. It might represent, to some extent, the circumstances of trade between the Channel Islands and the larger markets of England, though, of course, it is never fully verified, because the smallest purchasers do affect the market in some degree. The equation more accurately represents the position of a single trader with regard to the aggregate trade of a large community, since he must buy and sell at the current prices, which he cannot in an appreciable degree affect.

A still simpler formula, however, is needed to represent the conditions of a large part of our purchases. In many cases we want so little of a commodity, that an individual need not give more than a very small fraction of his possessions to obtain it. We may suppose, then, that y in the last problem was a very small part of c, so that $\psi_2(c-y)$ does not differ appreciably from $\psi_2 c$. Taking m as before to be the existing ratio of exchange, we have the one equation

$$\frac{\phi_2 x}{\psi_2 c} = m,$$

or $\phi_2 x = m. \psi_2 c.$

This means that C will buy of the commodity until its degree of utility falls below that of the commodity he gives. A person's expenditure on salt is an inconsiderable item of expense; what he spends thus does not make him appreciably poorer; yet, if the established price or ratio is one penny for each pound of salt, he buys in any time, say one year, so many pounds that an additional pound would not have so much utility to him as a penny. In the above equation $m. \psi_2 c$ represents the utility to him of a penny, an inconsiderable fraction of his possessions, and he buys salt until $\phi_2 x$, which is approximately the utility of the next pound, is equal to, or it may be somewhat less, than that of the penny. But this case must not be confused with that of purchases which appreciably affect the possessions of the purchaser. Thus, if a poor family purchase much butchers'-meat, they will probably have to go without something else. The more they buy, the lower the final degree of utility of the meat, and *the higher the final degree of utility of something else;* and thus these purchases will be the more narrowly limited.

Complex Cases of the Theory.

We have hitherto considered the Theory of Exchange as applying only to two trading bodies possessing and dealing in two commodities. Exactly the same principles hold true, however numerous and complicated the conditions. The main point to be remembered in tracing out the results of the theory is, that the same commodities in the same market can have only one ratio of exchange, which must therefore prevail between each body and each other, the costs of conveyance being considered as *nil.* The equations become rapidly more numerous as additional bodies or commodities are considered; but we may exhibit them in the case of three trading bodies and three commodities.

Thus, suppose that

A possesses the stock a of cotton, and gives
x_1 of it to B, x_2 to C.

B possesses the stock b of silk, and gives
y_1 to A, y_2 to C.

C possesses the stock c of wool, and gives
z_1 to A, z_2 to B.

We have here altogether six unknown quan-
tities—x_1, x_2, y_1, y_2, z_1, z_2; but we have also sufficient means of determining them. They are
exchanged as follows—

A gives x_1 for y_1, and x_2 for z_1.
B   „ y_1 for x_1, and y_2 for z_2.
C   „ z_1 for x_2, and z_2 for y_2.

These may be treated as independent exchanges;
each body must be satisfied in regard to each
of its exchanges, and we must therefore take
into account the functions of utility or the
final degrees of utility of each commodity in
respect of each body. Let us express these
functions as follows—

ϕ_1, ψ_1, χ_1 are the respective functions of
utility for . . . . . . A.
ϕ_2, ψ_2, χ_2 . . . . B.
ϕ_3, ψ_3, χ_3 . . . . C.

Now A, after the exchange, will hold $a - x_1 - x_2$
of cotton and y_1 of silk; and B will hold x_1 of

cotton and $b - y_1 - y_2$ of silk: their ratio of exchange, y_1 for x_1, will therefore be governed by the following pair of equations—

$$\frac{\phi_1 (a - x_1 - x_2)}{\psi_1 y_1} = \frac{y_1}{x_1} = \frac{\phi_2 x_1}{\psi_2 (b - y_1 - y_2)}.$$

The exchange of A with C will be similarly determined by the ratio of the degrees of utility of cotton and wool on each side subsequent to the exchange; hence we have

$$\frac{\phi_1 (a - x_1 - x_2)}{\chi_1 z_1} = \frac{z_1}{x_2} = \frac{\phi_3 x_2}{\chi_3 (c - z_1 - z_2)}.$$

There will also be interchange between B and C which will be independently regulated on similar principles, so that we have another pair of equations to complete the conditions, namely,

$$\frac{\psi_2 (b - y_1 - y_2)}{\chi_2 z_2} = \frac{z_2}{y_2} = \frac{\psi_2 y_2}{\chi_3 (c - z_1 - z_2)}.$$

We might proceed in the same way to lay down the conditions of exchange between more numerous bodies, but the principles would be exactly the same. For every quantity of commodity which is given something must be received; and if it be received from several parties, then we may conceive the quantity which is given for it to be broken up into as many distinct portions. The exchanges in the most complicated case may thus always be decom-

posed into simple exchanges, and every exchange will give rise to two equations sufficient
to determine the quantities involved. The same
can also be done when there are two or more
commodities in the possession of each trading
body.

One case of the Theory of Exchange is of
considerable importance, and arises when two
parties compete in supplying a third with a
certain commodity. Thus, suppose that A, with
the quantity of one commodity denoted by a,
purchases another kind of commodity both from
B and C, which respectively possess b and c of
it. All the quantities concerned are as follows—

A gives x_1 of a to B and x_2 to C,
B „ y_1 of b to A,
C „ y_2 of c to A.

As each commodity may be supposed to be
perfectly homogeneous, the ratio of exchange
must be the same in one case as in the other,
so that we have one equation thus furnished—

$$\frac{y_1}{x_1} = \frac{y_2}{x_2}.$$ (1)

Now, provided that A gets the right commodity in the proper quantity, he does not care
whence it comes, so that we need not, in his

equation, distinguish the source or destination of the quantities; he simply gives $x_1 + x_2$, and receives in exchange $y_1 + y_2$. Observing, then, that by (1)

$$\frac{y_1 + y_2}{x_1 + x_2} = \frac{y_1}{x_1}$$

we have the usual equation of exchange—

$$\frac{\phi_1 (a - x_1 - x_2)}{\psi_1 (y_1 + y_2)} = \frac{y_1}{x_1}. \tag{2}$$

But B and C must both be separately satisfied with their portions of the transaction. Thus

$$\frac{\phi_2 \, x_1}{\psi_2 (b - y_1)} = \frac{y_1}{x_1}; \tag{3}$$

$$\frac{\phi_3 \, x_2}{\psi_3 (c - y_2)} = \frac{y_2}{x_2}. \tag{4}$$

There are altogether four unknown quantities— x_1, x_2, y_1, y_2; and it is apparent that we have four equations by which to determine them. Various suppositions might be made as to the comparative magnitude of the quantities b and c, or the character of the functions concerned; and conclusions could then be drawn as to the effect upon the trade. The general result would be, that the smaller holder must more or less comform to the prices of the larger holder.

Failure of the Equations of Exchange.

Cases may readily occur in which equations of the kind set forth in the preceding pages fail to hold true, or lead to impossible results. Such failure may indicate that no exchange at all takes place, but it may also have a different meaning.

In the first place, it may happen that the commodity possessed by A has a high degree of utility to A, and a low degree to B, and that *vice versâ* B's commodity has a high degree of utility to B and less to A. This difference of utility might exist to such an extent, that though B were to receive very little of A's commodity, yet the final degree of utility to him would be less than that of his own commodity, of which he enjoys much more. In such a case no benefit can arise from exchange, and no exchange will consequently take place. This failure of exchange will be indicated by a failure of the equations.

But it may also happen that the whole quantities of commodity possessed are exchanged, and yet the equations fail. A may have so low a desire for consuming his own commodity, that the very last minute portion of it has less degree of utility to him than a small addition to the commodity received in exchange. The same state of things might happen to exist with B as regards his commodity: under these circumstances the whole possessions of one might be exchanged for the whole of the other, and the ratio of exchange would of course be defined by these quantities. Yet each party might desire the last increment of the commodity received more than the last increment of that given, so that the equations would fail to be true. This case will hardly occur practically in international trade, since two nations usually trade in many commodities, which would alter the conditions.

Again, the equations of exchange will fail to be possible when the commodity or useful article possessed on one or both sides is indivisible. We have always assumed hitherto that more or less of a commodity may be had, even down to infinitely small quantities. This is approximately true of all ordinary trade, especially international trade between great industrial nations. Any one sack of corn or any one bar of iron is practically infinitesimal compared with the quantities exchanged by America and England; and even one cargo or parcel of

corn or iron is an inconsiderable fraction of the
whole. But, in exceptional cases, even international trade might involve indivisible articles.
We might conceive the British Government
giving the Koh-i-noor diamond to the Khedive
of Egypt in exchange for Pompey's Pillar, in
which case it would certainly not answer the
purpose to break up one article or the other.
When an island or portion of territory is transferred from one possessor to another, it is
often necessary to take the whole, or none.
America, in purchasing Alaska from Russia,
would hardly have consented to purchase less
than the whole. In every sale of a house, factory, or other building, it is usually impractic-
able to make any division without greatly
lessening the utility of the whole. In all such
cases our equations must fail to exist, because
we cannot contemplate the existence of an
increment or a decrement to an indivisible
article.

Suppose, for example, that A and B each possess a book: they cannot break up the books,
and must therefore exchange them entire, if at
all. Under what conditions will they do so?
Plainly on the condition that each makes a gain
of utility by so doing. Here we deal not with

the final degree of utility depending on an infinitesimal quantity, but on the *whole utility of
the complete article.*   Now let

u_1 be the utility of A's book to A,

u_2 „   „   A's   „   to B,

v_1 „   „   B's   „   to A,

v_2 „   „   B's   „   to B.

Then the conditions of exchange are simply

$$v_1 > u_1,$$
$$u_2 > v_2.$$

We might indeed contemplate the case where
the utilities were exactly equal on one side ;
thus

$$v_1 > u_1,$$
$$u_2 = v_2.$$

B would then be wholly indifferent to any exchange, and I do not see any means of deciding
whether he would or would not consent to it.
But we need hardly consider the case, as it
could seldom practically occur.   Were the utilities exactly equal on both sides, there would
obviously be no motive to exchange.   Again,
the slightest loss of utility on either side would
be a complete bar to the transaction, because
we are not supposing, at present, that any other
commodities are in possession so as to allow of
separate inducements, or that any other motives
than such as arise out of commercial gain and

simple desire of one's own convenience enter into the question.

A much more difficult problem arises if we suppose an indivisible article exchanged for a divisible commodity. When Russia sold Alaska this was a practically indivisible thing, but it was bought with money of which more or less might be given to indefinitely small quantities. A bargain of this kind is exceedingly common; indeed it occurs in the case of every house, mansion, estate, factory, ship, or other complete whole, which is sold for money. Our former equations of exchange certainly fail, for they involve increments of commodity on both sides. The theory seems to give a very unsatisfactory answer, for the problem proves to be, within certain limits, indeterminate.

Let X be the indivisible article; u_1 its utility to its possessor A, and u_2 its utility to B. Let y be the quantity of commodity given for it, which may be in any degree more or less; let v_1 be the whole utility of y to A, and v_2 to B. Then it is quite evident that, to give rise to exchange, v_1 must be greater than u_1, and u_2 must be greater than v_2; that is, there must be a gain of utility on each side. The quantity y must not be so great as to deprive B of gain, nor so small as to deprive A of gain. The following is an extract from Mr. Thornton's work which exactly expresses the problem :—

'There are two opposite extremes—one above which the price of a commodity cannot rise, the other below which it cannot fall.' The upper of these limits is marked by the utility, real or supposed, of the commodity to the customer; the lower, of its utility to the dealer. No one will give for a commodity a quantity of money or money's worth, which, in his opinion, would be of more use to him than the commodity itself. No one will take for a commodity a quantity of money or of anything else which he thinks would be of less use to himself than the commodity. The price eventually given and taken may be either at one of the opposite extremes, or may be anywhere intermediate between them [e].'

Three distinct cases might occur which can best be illustrated by a concrete example. Suppose we can read the thoughts of the parties in the sale of a house. If A says £1200 is the least price which will give any gain, and B holds that £800 is the highest price which will

[e] Thornton 'On Labour ; its Wrongful · Claims and Rightful Dues' (1869), p. 58.

be profitable to him, no exchange can possibly take place. If A should find £1000 to be his lowest limit, while B happens to name the same sum for his highest limit, the transaction can be closed, and the price will be exactly defined. But supposing, finally, that A is really willing to sell at £900, and B is prepared to buy at £1100, in what manner can we theoretically determine the price? I see no mode of solving the question. Any price between £900 and £1100 will leave a profit on each side, and both parties will lose if they do not come to terms. I conceive that such a transaction must be settled upon other than economical grounds. The disposition and force of character of the parties, their comparative persistency, their adroitness and experience in business, or it may be a feeling of justice or of kindliness really influences the decision. These are motives altogether extraneous to a theory of Economy, and yet they appear necessary considerations in this problem. It may be, that indeterminate bargains of this kind are best arranged by an arbitrator or third party.

The equations of exchange may fail again where commodities are divisible, but not to indefinitely small quantities. There is always, in retail trade, a convenient unit below which we do not descend in purchases. Paper may be bought in quires, or even in packets, which it may not be desirable to break up. Wine cannot be bought from the wine merchant in less than a bottle at a time. In all such cases exchange cannot, theoretically speaking, be perfectly adjusted, because it will be infinitely improbable that an exact number of units will give exact equations of utility. In a large proportion of cases, indeed, the unit may be so small compared with the whole quantities exchanged, as practically to be indefinitely small. But suppose that a person be buying ink which is only to be had, under the circumstances, in one shilling bottles. If one bottle be not quite enough, how will he decide whether to take a second or not. Clearly by estimating the aggregate utility of the bottle of ink compared with the shilling. If there be an excess, he will certainly purchase it, and proceed to consider whether a third be desirable or not.

This case might be illustrated by Figure VI, in which the spaces oq_1, p_1q_2, p_2q_3, &c. repre-. sent the whole utility of successive bottles of ink; while the spaces or_1, p_1r_2, &c. equal in size to each other, represent the utility of successive

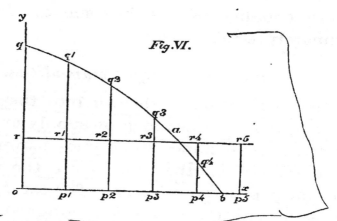

shillings. There is no doubt that three bottles
will be purchased, but the fourth will not be
purchased unless the space $p_3\ q_3\ q_4\ p_4$ exceed in
area $p_3\ r_3\ r_4\ p_4$.

Cases of this kind are similar to those treated
in p. 119, where the things exchanged are indivisible, except that the question of exchange
or no exchange occurs over and over again
with respect to each successive unit, and is
decided in respect to each by the excess of the
total utility of the unit received over the total
utility of that given. There is indeed perfect
harmony between the cases where equations
can and where they cannot be established; for
we have only to imagine the indivisible units
of commodity to be indefinitely lessened in size
to enable us to pass gradually down to the case

where equality of the increments of utility is ultimately established.

Equivalence of Commodities.

Much confusion is thrown into the statistical investigation of questions of supply and demand by the circumstance that one commodity can often replace another, and serve the same purpose more or less perfectly. The same, or nearly the same substance is often obtained from two or three sources. The constituents of wheat, barley, oats, and rye are closely similar, if not identical. Vegetable structures are composed mainly of the same chemical compound in nearly all cases. Animal meat, again, is of nearly the same composition from whatever animal derived. There are endless differences of flavour and quality, but these are often insufficient to prevent one kind from serving in place of another.

Whenever different commodities are thus applicable to the same purposes, their conditions of demand and exchange are not independent. Their mutual ratio of exchange cannot vary much, for it will be closely defined by the ratio of their utilities. Beef and mutton, for instance, differ so little, that many people eat them almost indifferently. The price of mutton, on an average, exceeds that of beef in the ratio of 9 to 8; we must conclude that people generally esteem mutton more than beef in this proportion, otherwise they would not buy the dearer meat. It follows, that the final degrees of utility of these meats are in this ratio, or that if ϕx be the degree of utility of mutton, and ψy that of beef, we have

$$\phi x = \tfrac{8}{8} \psi y.$$

This equation would doubtless not hold true in extreme circumstances; if mutton became comparatively scarce, there would probably be some persons willing to pay a higher price merely because it would then be considered a delicacy. But this is certain, that so long as the equation holds true, the ratio of exchange between mutton and beef will not diverge from that of 8 to 9. If the supply of beef falls off to a small extent, people will not pay a higher price for it, but will eat more mutton; and if the supply of mutton falls off, they will eat more beef. The conditions of supply will have no effect whatever upon the ratio of exchange; we must, in fact, treat beef and mutton as one commodity of two different strengths, just as gold at eighteen and twenty carats is hardly considered as two but as one commodity, of which twenty parts of one are equivalent to eighteen of the other.

It is upon this principle that we must explain, in harmony with Professor Cairnes' views, the extraordinary permanence of the ratio of exchange of gold and silver, which for several centuries past has never diverged much from 15 to 1. That this fixedness of ratio does not depend upon the amount or cost of production is proved by the very slight effect of the Australian and Californian gold discoveries, which never raised the gold price of silver more than about $4\frac{2}{3}$ per cent., and has failed to have a permanent effect of more than $1\frac{1}{2}$ per cent. It must be due to the fact, that gold and silver can be employed for exactly the same purposes, but that the superior brilliancy of gold occasions it to be preferred, unless it be about 15 or $15\frac{1}{2}$ times as costly as silver. Probably, however, the fixed ratio of $15\frac{1}{2}$ to 1, according to which these metals are exchanged in the currency of France and some other continental countries, has helped to render steady the market ratio of exchange of the metals. The French Currency Law of the Year XI establishes an artificial equation—

K

Utility of gold $=15\frac{1}{2}\times$ Utility of silver;
and it is probably not without some reason that
M. Wolowski and other recent French economists attributed to this law of replacement an
important effect in preventing disturbance in
the relations of gold and silver.

Acquired Utility of Commodities.

The Theory of Exchange, as explained above,
rests entirely on the consideration of quantities
of utility, and no reference to labour or cost of
production has been made.   The value of a
commodity, if I may for a moment use the dan-
gerous term, is measured, not by its total utility, but by the intensity of the need we have
for *more* of it.   But the power of exchanging
one commodity for another greatly extends the
range of this utility.   We are no longer limited
to considering the degree of utility of a commodity as regards the wants of its immediate possessor; for it may have a higher usefulness to
some other person, and can be transferred to
that person in exchange for some commodity
of superior utility to the purchaser.   The general result of exchange is, that all commodities
sink, as it were, to the same level of utility in
respect of the last portions consumed.

In the Theory of Exchange we find that the possessor of any divisible commodity will exchange such a portion of it, that the next increment would have exactly equal utility with the increment of other produce which he would receive for it. This will hold good however various may be the kinds of commodity he requires. Suppose that a person possesses one single commodity, which we may consider to be money, or income, and that p, q, r, s, t, &c. are quantities of other commodities which he purchases with portions of his income. Let x be the uncertain quantity of money which he will desire not to exchange; what relation will exist between these quantities x, p, q, r, &c. ? This relation will partly depend upon the ratio of exchange, partly on the final degree of utility of these commodities. Let us assume, for a moment, that all the ratios of exchange are equalities, or that a unit of one is always to be purchased with a unit of another. Then, plainly, we must have the degrees of utility equal, otherwise there would be advantage in acquiring more of that possessing the higher degree of utility. Let the sign ϕ denote the function of utility, which will be different in each case; then we have simply the equations—

$$\phi_1\,x = \phi_2\,p = \phi_3\,q = \phi_4\,r = \phi_5\,s = \&c.$$

But, as a matter of fact, the ratios of exchange are seldom or never that of unit for unit; and when the quantities exchanged are unequal, the degrees of utility will not be equal. If for one pound of silk I can have three of cotton, then the degree of utility of cotton must be a third that of silk, otherwise I should gain by exchange. Thus the general result of the facility of exchange prevailing in a civilized country is, that *a person procures such quantities of commodities that the final degrees of utility are inversely as the ratios of exchange of the commodities.*

Let x_1, x_2, x_3, x_4, &c. be the portions of his income given for p, q, r, s, &c. respectively, then we must have

$$\frac{\phi_2\,p}{\phi_1\,x} = \frac{x_1}{p}, \qquad \frac{\phi_3\,q}{\phi_1\,x} = \frac{x_2}{q}, \qquad \frac{\phi_4\,r}{\phi_1\,x} = \frac{x_3}{r},$$

and so on. The theory thus represents the fact, that a person distributes his expenditure in such a way as to equalise the utility of the final increments in each branch of expenditure. This distribution will greatly vary with different individuals, but it is self-evident that the want which an individual feels most acutely at the moment will be that upon which he will expend some of his income if possible.

It will be seen that we can now conceive, in an accurate manner, the utility of money, or of the supply of commodity which forms a person's livelihood. Its final degree of utility is measured by that of any of the other commodities which he consumes. What, for instance, is the utility of one penny to a poor family earning fifty pounds a year? As a penny is an inconsiderable portion of their income, it may represent one of the indefinitely small increments, and its utility is equal to the utility of the quantity of bread, tea, sugar, or other articles which they could purchase with it, this utility depending upon the extent to which they were already provided with those articles. To a family possessing one thousand pounds a year, the utility of a penny may be measured in an exactly similar manner; but it will be found to be much less, because their want of any given commodity will be satiated or satisfied to a much greater extent, so that the urgency of need for a pennyworth more of any article is much reduced.

The general result of exchange is thus to produce a certain equality of utility between different commodities, as regards the same individual; but between different individuals no

such equality will exist. In Political Economy
we regard only commercial transactions, and no
equalisation of wealth from charitable motives
is considered. The utility of wealth to a very
rich man will be governed by its utility in that
branch of expenditure in which he continues
to feel the most need of more possessions. His
primary wants will long since have been fully
satisfied; he could find food, if requisite, for a
thousand persons, and so, of course, he will have
supplied himself with as much as he in the least
desires. But so far as is consistent with the
inequality of wealth in every community, all
commodities are distributed in exchange so as
to produce the maximum of benefit. Every person whose wish for a certain thing exceeds his
wish for other things, acquires what he wants,
provided he can make a sufficient sacrifice in
other respects. No one is ever required to give
what he more desires for what he less desires,
so that perfect freedom of exchange must be to
the advantage of all.

The Advantage of Exchange.

It is a most important deduction from this
theory that the ratio of exchange gives no indi-
cation of the real benefit derived from the act

of exchange. So many trades are occupied in buying and selling, and depend for their profit upon buying low and selling high, that there arises a fallacious tendency to believe that the whole benefit of trade is in low prices. It is implied that to pay a high price is worse than doing without the article, and the whole financial system of a great nation may be distorted in the effort to carry out a false theory.

This is the result to which some of Mr. Mill's remarks, in his 'Theory of International Trade,' would lead. That theory is always ingenious, and nearly always, as it seems to me, true ; but he draws from it the following conclusion [f] :—
'The countries which carry on their foreign trade on the most advantageous terms, are those whose commodities are most in demand by foreign countries, and which have themselves the least demand for foreign commodities. From which, among other consequences, it follows, that the richest countries, *cæteris paribus,* gain the least by a given amount of foreign commerce : since, having a greater demand for commodities generally, they are likely to have a greater demand for foreign commodities, and thus modify the terms of interchange

[f] 'Principles of Political Economy,' book iii. chap. 18, § 8.

to their own disadvantage. Their aggregate gains by foreign trade, doubtless, are generally greater than those of poorer countries, since they carry on a greater amount of such trade, and gain the benefit of cheapness on a larger consumption ; -but their gain is less on each individual article consumed.'

In the absence of any explanation, this passage must be taken to mean, that the advantage of foreign trade depends upon the terms of exchange, and that international trade is less advantageous to a rich than to a poor country. But such a conclusion involves a confusion between two distinct things—the price of a commodity and its total utility. A country is not merely like a great mercantile firm buying and selling goods and making a profit out of the difference of price ; it buys goods in order to consume them. But, in estimating the benefit a consumer derives from a commodity, it is the total utility which must be taken as the measure, not the final degree of utility on which the terms of exchange depend.

To illustrate this we may employ the curves in Figure VII to represent the functions of utility of two commodities. Let the wool of Australia be represented by the line *ob*, and its

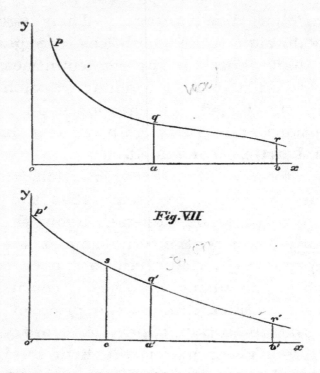

Fig. VII

total utility to Australia by the area of the curvilinear figure *obrp*. Let the utility of a second commodity, say cotton goods, to Australia be similarly represented in the lower curve, so that the quantity of commodity measured by *o'b'* gives a total utility represented by the figure *o'p'q'b'*. Then, if Australia gives half its wool, *ab*, for the quantity of cotton goods represented by *o'a'*, it loses the utility *aqrb*, but gains that represented by the larger area *o'p'q'a'*. There is accordingly a considerable net gain of utility which is the real object of exchange. Even had Australia sold its wool at a lower price, obtaining cotton goods only to the amount of $o'c$, the utility of this amount, $op'sc$, would have exceeded that of the wool given for it. A prohibitory tariff in the case of Australia would have a most fatal effect in preventing the country from enjoying the high utility of goods manufactured in Europe with centuries of experience.

So far is Mr. Mill's statement from being fundamentally correct, that I should be inclined to make the opposite statement, namely, that the greatness of the price which a country is willing to pay for the productions of other countries marks the greatness of the benefit which it derives from the trade. He who pays a high price must either have a very great need of that which he buys, or very little of that which he pays for it; and, on either supposition, there is gain by exchange. In questions of this sort there is, I believe, but one rule which can be safely laid down, that no one will buy a thing unless he feels advantage from the purchase; and perfect freedom of exchange, therefore, tends to the maximising of utility.

One advantage of the Theory of Political Economy, carefully studied, will be to make us very careful in many of our conclusions. The fact that we can most imperfectly estimate the total utility of any one commodity should prevent our attempting to measure the benefit of any trade. Accordingly, when Mr. Mill proceeds from his theory of international trade to that of taxation, and arrives at the conclusion that one nation may, by means of taxes on commodities imported, ' appropriate to itself, at the expense of foreigners, a larger share than would otherwise belong to it of the increase in the general productiveness of the labour and capital of the world g,' I venture entirely to question the truth of his results. I conceive that his arguments involve a confusion between the ratio of exchange and the total utility of a commodity, and a far more accurate knowledge of economical laws than any one yet possesses would be required to estimate the true effect of any tax. While customs duties may in some cases be defensible as a means of raising revenue, the time is past when any economist should give the slightest countenance to their employment for manipulating trade, or interfering with the natural tendency of exchange to increase utility.

g ' Principles of Political Economy,' book v. chap. 4, § 6.

Mode of ascertaining the Variation of Utility.

The future progress of Political Economy as a strict science must greatly depend upon our acquiring more accurate notions of the variable quantities concerned in the problem. We cannot really tell the effect of any change in trade or manufacture until we can with some approach to truth express the laws of the variation of utility numerically. To do this we need accurate statistics of the quantities of commodities purchased by the whole population at various prices. The price of a commodity is the only test we have of the utility of the commodity to the purchaser; and if we could tell exactly how much people reduce their consumption of each important article when the price rises, we could determine, at least approximately, the variation of the final degree of utility—the all-important element in Economy.

In such calculations we may often make use of the simpler equation given on p 112. For the first approximation we may assume that the general utility of a person's income is not affected by the changes of price of the commodity; so that if, in the equation

$$\phi\, x = m \,.\, \psi\, c$$

we have many different corresponding values for x and m, we may treat ψc, the utility of money, as a constant, and determine the general character of the function ϕx, the final degree of utility. This function would doubtless be a purely empirical one—a mere aggregate of terms devised so that their sum shall vary in accordance with statistical facts. The subject is too complex to allow of our expecting any simple compact law like that of gravity. Nor, when we have got the laws, shall we be able to give any exact explanation of them. They will be of the same character as the empirical formulæ used in the science of Meteorology [h], mere aggregates of mathematical symbols intended to replace a tabular statement, except that they will not be periodic. Nevertheless, their determination will render Economy a science as exact as many of the purely physical sciences; as exact, for instance, as Meteorology is likely to be for a very long time to come.

The method of determining the function of utility explained above will hardly apply, however, to the main elements of expenditure. The

[h] Sir J. Herschel's ' Meteorology,' Encyclopædia Britannica, §§ 143–157.

price of bread, for instance, cannot be properly
brought under the equation used, because, when
the price of bread rises much, the resources of
poor persons are strained, money becomes
scarcer with them, and ψc, the utility of
money, rises. The natural result is, the lessening of expenditure in other directions; that is
to say, all the wants of a poor person are supplied to a less degree of satisfaction when food
is dear than when it is cheap. It is difficult to
see exactly how we are to disentangle these
effects and determine the variation of ψc. The
first step, no doubt, would be to ascertain what
proportion of the expenditure of poor people
goes to food, at various prices of that food.
Great difficulty is thrown in the way of all
such inquiries by the vast differences in the
condition of persons.

*Opinions of Economists on the Variation of
Price.*

There is no difficulty in finding, in works of
Political Economists, remarks upon the relation
between any change in the supply of a commodity and the consequent rise of price. The
general principles of the variation of utility
have been familiar to many writers.

As a general rule the variation of price is much more marked in the case of necessaries of life than in the case of luxuries. This result would follow from the fact observed by Adam Smith, that 'The desire for food is limited in every man by the narrow capacity of the human stomach; but the desire of the conveniences and ornaments of building, dress, equipage, and household furniture, seems to have no limit or certain boundary.' As I assert that value depends upon desire for more, it follows that any excessive supply of food will lower its price very much more than in the case of articles of luxury. Reciprocally a deficiency of food will raise its price much more than would happen in the case of less necessary articles. This conclusion is in harmony with facts; for Chalmers says[i]: 'The necessaries of life are far more powerfully affected in the price of them by a variation in their quantity, than are the luxuries of life.' Let the crop of grain be deficient by one-third in its usual amount, or rather, let the supply of grain in the market, whether from the home produce, or by importation, be curtailed to the same extent, and this will create

[i] Chalmers' 'Christian and Economic Polity of a Nation,' vol. ii. p. 240.

a much greater addition than of one-third to the price of it. It is not an unlikely prediction, that its cost would be more than doubled by the shortcoming of one-third or one-fourth in the supply.' He goes on to explain, at considerable length, that the same would not happen with such an article as *rum*. A deficiency in the supply of rum from the West Indies would occasion a rise of price, but not to any great extent, because there would be a substitution of other kinds of spirits, or else a reduction in the amount consumed. Men can live without luxuries, but not without necessaries. ' A failure in the general supply of esculents to the extent of one-half, would more than quadruple the price of the first necessaries of life, and would fall with very aggravated pressure on the lower orders. A failure to the same extent in all the vineyards of the world, would most assuredly not raise the price of wine to anything near this proportion. Rather than pay four times the wonted price for Burgundy, there would be a general descent to claret, or from that to port, or from that to the home-made wines of our own country, or from that to its spirituous, or from that to its fermented

liquors [k].'   He points to sugar especially as an
article which would be extensively thrown out
of consumption by any great rise in price [l],
because it is a luxury, and at the same time
forms a considerable element in expenditure.
But he thinks that, if an article occasions a
total expenditure of very small amount, variations of price will not much affect consumption.
Speaking of nutmeg, he says :—

'There is not sixpence a year consumed of
it for each family in Great Britain ; and perhaps not one family that spends more than a
guinea on this article alone.   Let the price
then be doubled or trebled ; this will have
no perceptible effect on the demand ; and the
price will far rather be paid, than that the
wonted indulgence should in any degree be
foregone. . . . . The same holds true of cloves,
and cinnamon, and Cayenne pepper, and all the
precious spiceries of the East ; and it is thus,
that while, in the general, the price of necessaries differs so widely from that of luxuries,
in regard to the extent of oscillation, there
is a remarkable approximation in this matter

---

[k] Chalmers' 'Christian and Economic Polity of a Nation,'
vol. ii. p. 242.   [l] *Ibid*. p. 251.

between the very commonest of these necessaries and the very rarest of these luxuries m.'

In these interesting observations Chalmers
correctly distinguishes between the effect of
desire for the commodity in question and that
for other commodities. The price of nutmeg
does not appreciably affect the general supply
of other things, and the equation on p. 112 therefore correctly applies. But if sugar be scarce,
to consume as before would necessitate a reduction of consumption in other directions; and as
the degree of utility of more necessary articles
rises much more rapidly than that of sugar, it
is the latter article which is thrown out of use
by preference. This is a far more complex
case, which includes also the case of corn and
all large articles of consumption.

Dr. Chalmers' remarks on the price of sugar
are strongly supported by facts concerning the
course of the sugar markets in 1855–6. In the
year 1855, as is stated in Tooke's 'History of
Prices [n],' attention was suddenly drawn to a
considerable reduction which had taken place
in the stocks of sugar. The price rapidly ad-
vanced, but before it had reached the highest

m Chalmers' 'Christian and Economic Polity of a Nation,'
vol. ii. p. 252.   n Vol. v. p. 324, &c.

point the demand became almost wholly suspended. Not only did retail dealers avoid replenishing their stocks, but there was an immediate and sometimes entire cessation of consumption among extensive classes. There were instances among the retail grocers of their not selling a single pound of sugar until prices receded to what the public was satisfied was a reasonable rate.

It is very curious that in this subject, which reaches to the very foundations of Political Economy, we owe more to early than later writers. Before our science could be said to exist at all, writers on Political Arithmetic had got quite as far as we at present are. In a pamphlet of 1737 [o], it is remarked that ' People who understand trade will readily agree with me, that the tenth part of a commodity in a market, more than there is a brisk demand for, is apt to lower the market, perhaps, twenty or thirty per cent.; and that a deficiency of a tenth part will cause as exorbitant an advance.' Sir J. Dalrymple [p], again, says :—

' Merchants observe, that if the commodity in market is diminished one-third beneath its mean quantity, it will be nearly doubled in value;

[o] Quoted by Lord Lauderdale.   [p] *Ibid.*

and that if it is augmented one-third above its mean quantity, it will sink near one-half in its value; or that, by further diminishing or augmenting the quantity, these disproportions between the quantity and prices vastly increase.'

To the 'Spectator ᵟ,' again, we owe the conjecture, that the production of one-tenth part more grain than is usually consumed would diminish the value of the grain one-half. I know nothing more strange and discreditable to statists and economists, than that in so important a point as the relations of price and supply of the main article of food, we owe our most accurate accounts to writers who lived from a century and a half to two centuries ago. There is a certain celebrated estimate of the variation of the price of corn which I have found quoted in innumerable works on Economy. It is commonly attributed to Gregory King, whose name should be held in honour as one of the fathers of Statistical Science in England. Born at Lichfield in 1648, King devoted himself much to mathematical studies, and was often occupied in surveying. His principal public appointments were that of Lancaster Herald and

---

ᵟ No. 200, quoted by Lauderdale.   'Inquiry into Public Wealth,' second edition, pp. 50, 51.

Secretary to the Commissioners of Public Accounts ; but he is known to fame by the remarkable statistical tables concerning the population and trade of England, which he completed in the year 1696. His treatise was entitled ' Natural and Political Observations and Conclusions upon the State and Condition of England, 1696 '; but was never printed in the author's lifetime. The contents were, however, communicated in the most liberal manner to Dr. Davenant, who founded thereupon his ' Essay upon the Probable Methods of making a People gainers in the Balance of Trade[r],' making suitable acknowledgments as to the source of his information. Our knowledge of Gregory King's conclusions was derived from this and other essays of Davenant, until Chalmers printed the whole treatise at the end of the third edition of his well-known ' Estimate of the Comparative Strength of Great Britain.'

The estimate of which I am about to speak is given by Davenant in the following words[s] :—

' We take it, that a defect in the harvest may raise the price of corn in the following proportions :

[r] ' The Political and Commercial Works of Charles Davenant,' vol. ii. p. 163.　　　　　[s] *Ibid,* p. 224.

Defect.		Above the Common Rate.
1 Tenth		3 Tenths
2 Tenths	raises	8 Tenths
3 Tenths	the	1.6 Tenths
4 Tenths	price	2.8 Tenths
5 Tenths		4.5 Tenths.

So that when corn rises to treble the common rate, it may be presumed that we want above $\frac{1}{3}$ of the common produce; and if we should want $\frac{5}{10}$, or half the common produce, the price would rise to near five times the common rate.'

Though this estimate has been always attributed to Gregory King, it is right to add, that I cannot find it in his published treatise; nor does Dr. Davenant, who elsewhere makes full acknowledgments of what he owes to King, here attribute it to his friend. It is therefore, perhaps, due to Davenant.

We may re-state this estimate in the following manner, taking the average harvest and the average price of corn as unity—

Quantity of Corn.		Prices.
1.0	.. ..	1.0
.9	.. ..	1.3
.8	.. ..:	1.8
.7	.. ..	2.6
.6	.. ..	3.8
.5	.. ..	5.5.

Many writers have commented on this estimate. Thornton [t] observes, that it is probably exceedingly inaccurate, and that it is not clear whether the total stock, or only the harvest of a single year, is to be taken as deficient. Tooke [u], however, than whom on such a point there would be no higher authority, believes that Gregory King's estimate 'is not very wide of the truth, from observation of the repeated occurrence of the fact that the price of corn in this country has risen from one hundred to two hundred per cent. and upwards when the utmost computed deficiency of the crops has not been more than between one-sixth and one-third of an average.'

I have endeavoured to ascertain the law to which Davenant's figures conform, and the mathematical function obtained does not greatly differ from what we might have expected. It is probable that the price of corn should never sink to zero, as, if abundant, it could be used for feeding horses, poultry, and cattle, or for other purposes for which it is too costly at present. It is said that in America corn has

t 'An Inquiry into the Nature and Effects of the Paper Credit of Great Britain,' pp. 270, 271.

u 'History of Prices,' vol. i. pp. 13—15.

been occasionally used as fuel. On the other hand, when the quantity is much diminished, the price should rise rapidly, and should become infinite before the quantity is zero, because famine would then be impending. The substitution of potatoes and other food renders the famine point very uncertain; but I think that a total deficiency of corn could not be made up by other food. Now a function of the form $\dfrac{a}{(x-b)^n}$ fulfils these conditions; for it becomes infinite when x is reduced to b, but for greater values of x always decreases as x increases. An inspection of the figures shows that n is probably about equal to 2, and assuming it as such, I have found that the most probable values of a and b are—

$$a = .824 \qquad\qquad b = .12.$$

The formula thus becomes

$$\text{price of corn} = \frac{.824}{(x - .12)^2},$$

$$\text{or approximately,} = \frac{5}{6(x - \frac{1}{8})^2}.$$

The following numbers show the degree of approximation between the first of these formulæ and the data of Davenant—

Harvest	1.0	.9	.8	.7	.6	.5
Price (Davenant)	1.0	1.3	1.8	2.6	3.8	5.5
Price calculated ..	1.06	1.36	1.78	2.45	3.58	5.71.

I cannot undertake to say how near Davenant's estimate agrees with experience; but, considering the close approximation in the above numbers, we may safely substitute the empirical formula $\dfrac{5}{6\,(x-\frac{1}{8})^2}$ for his numbers; and there are other reasons already stated for supposing that this formula is not far from the truth.

There is further reason for believing that the price of corn varies more rapidly than in the inverse ratio of the quantity. Mr. Tooke estimates [x] that in 1795 and 1796 the farmers of England gained seven millions sterling in each year by a deficiency of one-eighth part in the wheat crop, not including the considerable profit on the rise of price of other agricultural produce. In each of the years 1799 and 1800, again, farmers probably gained eleven millions sterling by deficiency. If the price of wheat varied inversely as the quantity, they would neither gain nor lose, and the fact that they gained agrees with our formula given above.

[x] ' History of Prices.'

The variation of utility has not been overlooked by mathematicians, who had observed, as long ago as the early part of last century, before, in fact, there was any science of Political Economy at all, that the theory of probabilities could not be applied to commerce or gaming without taking notice of the very different utility of the same sum of money to different persons. Suppose that an even and fair bet is made between two persons, one of whom has £10,000 a year, the other £100 a year; let it be an equal chance whether they gain or lose £50. The rich person will, in neither case, feel much difference; but the poor person will receive far more harm by losing £50 than he can be benefited by gaining it. The utility of money to a poor person varies rapidly with the amount; to a rich person less so. Daniel Bernouilli, accordingly, distinguished between the *moral expectation* in any question of probabilities and the *mathematical expectation*,—the latter being the simple chance of obtaining some possession, the former the chance combined with its utility to the person. Having no means of ascertaining numerically the variation of utility, Bernouilli had to make various assumptions of an arbitrary kind, and was then able to obtain reasonable answers to many important questions. It is almost self-evident that the utility of money decreases as a person's total wealth increases; if this be granted, it follows at once that gaming is, in the long run, a sure loss; that every person should, when possible, divide risks, that is, prefer two equal chances of £50 to one similar chance of £100; and the advantage of insurance of all kinds is proved from the same theory. Laplace drew a similar distinction between the *fortune physique*, the actual amount of a person's income, and the *fortune morale*, or its benefit to him ʸ.'

On the Origin of Value.

The preceding pages contain, if I am not mistaken, an explanation of the nature of value which will, for the most part, harmonise with previous views upon the subject. Ricardo has stated, like most other economists, that utility is absolutely essential to value; but that ' possessing utility, commodities derive their exchangeable value from two sources : from their scarcity, and from the quantity of labour re-

ʸ Todhunter's 'History of the Theory of Probability,' chap. xi. &c.

quired to obtain them ᶻ.' Senior, again, has admirably defined wealth, or objects possessing value, as ' those things, and those things only, which are transferable, are limited in supply, and are directly or indirectly productive of pleasure or preventive of pain.' Speaking only of things which are transferable, or capable of being passed from hand to hand, we find that the two clearest statements of the nature of value available, recognise *utility* and *scarcity* as the requisites. But the moment that we distinguish between the total utility of a mass of commodity and the degree of utility of different portions, we may say that the scarcity is that which prevents the fall in the final degree of utility. Bread has the almost infinite utility of maintaining life, and when it becomes a question of life or death, a small quantity of food exceeds in value all other things. But when we enjoy our ordinary supplies of food, a loaf of bread has little value, because the utility of an additional loaf is small, our appetite being satiated by our customary meals.

I have pointed out the excessive ambiguity of the word Value, and the apparent impossi-

---

ᶻ 'Principles of Political Economy and Taxation,' third edition, p. 2.

bility of safely using it. When used to express the mere fact of certain articles exchanging in a particular ratio, I have proposed to substitute the unequivocal expression—*ratio of exchange.* But I am inclined to believe that a ratio is not the meaning which most persons attach to the word Value. There is a certain sense of esteem, of desirableness, which we may have with regard to a thing apart from any distinct consciousness of the ratio in which it would exchange for other things. I may suggest that this distinct feeling of value is probably identical with the final degree of utility. While Adam Smith's often quoted *value in use* is the total utility of a commodity to us, the *value in exchange* is defined by the *terminal utility*, the remaining desire which we or others have for possessing more.

There remains the question of labour as an element of value. There have not been wanting economists who put forward labour as the *cause of value*, asserting that all objects derive their value from the fact that labour has been expended on them; and it is even implied, if not stated, that value will be exactly proportional to labour. This is a doctrine which cannot stand for a moment, being directly opposed to facts.   Ricardo disposes of such an opinion when he says[a] : 'There are some commodities, the value of which is determined by their scarcity alone.   No labour can increase the quantity of such goods, and therefore their value cannot be lowered by an increased supply.   Some rare statues and pictures, scarce books and coins, wines of a peculiar quality, which can only be made from grapes grown on a particular soil, of which there is a very limited quantity, are all of this description.   Their value is wholly independent of the quantity of labour originally necessary to produce them, and varies with the varying wealth and inclinations of those who are desirous to possess them.'

The mere fact that there are many things, such as rare ancient books, coins, antiquities, which have high values, and which are absolutely incapable of production now, disperses the notion that value depends on labour.   Even those things which are producible in any quantities by labour seldom exchange exactly at the corresponding values.   The market price of corn, cotton, iron, and most other things is, in the prevalent theories of value, allowed to

a 'Principles of Political Economy and Taxation,' third edition, p. 2.

fluctuate above or below its natural or cost value. There may, again, be any discrepancy between the quantity of labour spent upon an object and the value ultimately attaching to it. A great undertaking like the Great Western Railway, or the Thames Tunnel, may embody a vast amount of labour, but its value depends entirely upon the number of persons who find it useful. If no use could be found for the Great Eastern steam ship, its value would be *nil*, except for the utility of some of its materials. On the other hand, a successful undertaking, which happens to possess great utility, may have a value for a time, at least, far exceeding what has been spent upon it, as in the case of the Atlantic cable. The fact is, that *labour once spent has no influence on the future value of any article* : it is gone and lost for ever. In commerce, by-gones are for ever by-gones; and we are always starting clear at each moment, judging the values of things with a view to future utility. Industry is essentially prospective, not retrospective; and seldom does the result of any undertaking exactly coincide with the first intentions of its founders.

But though labour is never the cause of value, it is in a large proportion of cases the determining circumstance, and in the following way :—Value depends solely on the final degree of utility.   How can we vary this degree of utility ?—By having more or less of the commodity to consume.   And how shall we get more or less of it ?—By spending more or less labour in obtaining a supply.—According to this view, then, there are two-steps-between—labour and value.   Labour affects supply, and supply affects the degree of utility, which governs value, or the ratio of exchange.

But it is easy to go too far in considering labour as the regulator of value ; it is equally to be remembered that labour is itself of unequal value.   Ricardo, by a violent assumption, founded his theory of value on quantities of labour considered as one uniform thing.   He was aware that labour differs infinitely in quality and efficiency, so that each kind is more or less scarce, and is consequently paid at a higher or lower rate of wages.   He regarded these differences as disturbing circumstances which would have to be allowed for ; but his theory rests on the assumed equality of labour.   This theory rests on a wholly different ground.   I hold labour to be *essentially variable, so that its value must be determined by the value of the produce, not the value of the produce by that of the labour.* I hold it to be impossible to compare *à priori* the productive powers of a navvy, a carpenter, an iron-puddler, a schoolmaster, and a barrister. Accordingly, it will be found that not one of my equations represents a comparison between one man's labour and another's. The equation, if there is one at all, is between the same person in two or more different occupations. The subject is one in which complicated action and re-action takes place, and which we must defer until after we have described, in the next chapter, the Theory of Labour.

CHAPTER V.

THEORY OF LABOUR.

Definition of Labour.

As Adam Smith said,

' The real price of everything, what everything really costs to the man who wants to
acquire it, is the toil and trouble of acquiring
it. . . . . Labour was the first price, the
original purchase-money, that was paid for all
things [a].'

Labour is the beginning of the processes
treated by economists, as consumption is the
end and purpose. Labour is the painful exertion which we undergo to ward off pains of
greater amount, or to procure pleasures which
leave a balance in our favour. Courcelle-

---

[a] ' Wealth of Nations,' book i. chap. 5.

Seneuil [b] and Hearn have stated the problem of Economy with the utmost truth and brevity in saying, that it is *to satisfy our wants with the least sum of labour.*

In defining *labour* for the purposes of the economist we have a choice of two courses: we may, if we like, include in it *all exertion of body or mind.* A game of cricket would, in this sense, be labour; but if it be undertaken solely for the sake of the enjoyment attaching to it, we need scarcely take it under our notice. All exertion not directed to a distant and distinct end must necessarily be repaid simultaneously. There is no account of good or evil to be balanced at a future time. We are not prevented in any way from including such cases in our Theory of Economy; in fact, our Theory of Labour will, of necessity, apply to them. But we need not occupy our attention by cases which demand no calculus. When we exert ourselves for the sole amusement of the moment, there is but one rule needed, namely, to stop when we feel inclined—when the pleasure no longer equals the pain.

It will probably be better, therefore, to con-

b 'Traité Theorique et Pratique d'Economie Politique,' 2nd edition, vol. i. p. 33.

centrate our attention on such exertion as is only subsequently repaid. This agrees exactly with Say's definition of labour as ' *Action suivée, dirigée vers un but.*' (Labour, <u>I should say, is *any painful exertion of body or mind undergone with the view to future good.*</u> It is true that labour may be both agreeable and conducive to future good; but it is only agreeable in a limited amount, and most men are compelled by their wants to exert themselves longer and more severely than they would otherwise do.) When a labourer is inclined to stop, he clearly feels something that is irksome, and our theory will only involve the point where the exertion has become so painful as to nearly balance all other considerations. Whatever there is that is wholesome or agreeable about labour before it reaches this point may be taken as a net profit of good to the labourer; but it does not enter into the problem. It is only when labour becomes effort that we take account of it, and, as Hearn truly says [c], 'such effort, as the very term seems to imply, is more or less troublesome.' In fact, we must, as will shortly appear, measure labour by the amount of pain which attaches to it.

[c] 'Plutology,' p. 24.

Quantitative Notions of Labour.

Let us endeavour to form a clear notion of what we mean by amount of labour. It is plain that duration will be one element of it; for a person labouring *uniformly* during two months must be allowed to labour twice as much as during one month. But labour may vary also in intensity. In the same time a man may walk a greater or less distance; may saw a greater or less amount of timber; may pump a greater or less quantity of water; in short, may exert more or less muscular force. Hence amount of labour will be a quantity of two dimensions, the product of intensity and time when the intensity is uniform, or the sum represented by the area of a curve when it is variable. But the intensity of labour may have more than one meaning; it may be measured by the quantity of work done, or by the painfulness of the effort of doing it. These two circumstances must be carefully distinguished, and both are of great importance for the theory. The one is the reward, the other the penalty, of labour. And, indeed, as the produce is only of interest to us so far as it possesses utility, we may say that there are three quantities involved in a problem of labour—the amount of painful exertion, the amount of produce, and the amount of utility. The variation of utility, as depending on the quantity of commodity possessed, has already been considered ; the variation of the amount of produce will be treated in the next chapter; we will here give attention to the law of the painfulness of labour.

(Abundant experience shows that as labour is prolonged the effort becomes rapidly more and more painful. A few hours' work per day may be considered agreeable rather than otherwise; but so soon as the spontaneous energy of the body is drained off, it becomes irksome to remain at work. As complete exhaustion approaches, continued effort becomes more and more intolerable.) Mr. Jennings has so clearly stated this law of the variation of labour, that I must quote his words [d]. 'Between these two points, the point of incipient effort and the point of painful suffering, it is quite evident that the degree of toilsome sensations endured does not vary directly as the quantity of work performed, but increases much more rapidly, like the resistance offered by an opposing medium to the velocity of a moving body.

[d] 'Natural Elements of Political Economy,' p. 119.

'When this observation comes to be applied
to the toilsome sensations endured by the working classes, it will be found convenient to fix
on a middle point, the average amount of toilsome sensation attending the average amount
of labour, and to measure from this point the
degrees of variation. If, for the sake of illustration, this average amount be assumed to be
of ten hours duration, it would follow that, if
at any period the amount were to be supposed
to be reduced to five hours, the sensations of
labour would be found, at least by the majority
of mankind, to be almost merged in the pleasures of occupation and exercise, whilst the
amount of work performed would only be diminished by one half; if, on the contrary, the
amount were to be supposed to be increased
to twenty hours, the quantity of work produced
would only be doubled, whilst the amount of
toilsome suffering would become insupportable.
Thus, if the quantity produced, greater or less
than the average, were to be divided into any
number of parts of equal magnitude, the amount
of toilsome sensation attending each succeeding
increment would be found greater than that
which would attend the increment preceding;
and the amount attending each succeeding de-

crement would be found less than that which
would attend the decrement preceding.'

There can be no question of the general truth
of the statement, although we may not have
the data for assigning the exact law of the
variation. (We may imagine the painfulness
of labour in proportion to produce to be re-

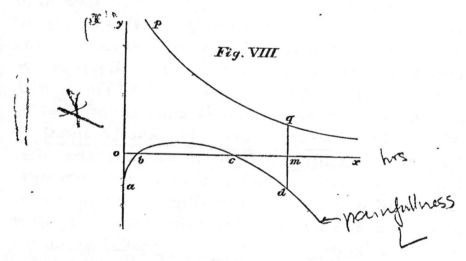

Fig. VIII

presented by some such curve as *abcd* in Fig.
VIII.   In this diagram the height of points
above the line *ox* denotes pleasure, and depth
below it pain.) At the moment of commencing
labour it is always more irksome than when
the mind and body are well bent to the work.
Thus, at first, the pain is measured by *oa*.   At
b there is neither pain nor pleasure.   Between

b and c (a small excess of pleasure is represented as due to the exertion itself.) But after c the energy begins to be rapidly exhausted, and the resulting pain is shown by the increasing tendency downwards of the line cd.   But we may at the same time (represent the utility of the produce by some such curve as pq, the amount of produce, or the day's wages,) being measured along the line ox. (Agreeably to the theory of utility, already given, the curve shows that the larger the wages earned the less is the pleasure derived from a further increment.) There will, of necessity, be some point m such that $qm = dm$, where the pleasure gained is exactly equal to the labour endured. (Now, if we pass the least beyond this point, a balance of pain will result : there will be an ever-decreasing motive in favour of labour, and an ever-increasing motive against it.) The labourer will evidently cease, then, at the point m. It would be inconsistent with human nature for a man to work when the pain of work exceeds the desire of possession, and all the motives for exertion.

We usually consider the duration of labour as measured by the number of hours' work per day.   The alternation of day and night on the earth has rendered man essentially periodic in his habits and actions. In a natural or wholesome condition a man must be considered as returning each twenty-four hours to exactly the same state ; or, at any rate, the cycle must be closed within the seven days. Thus the labourer must not be supposed to be either increasing or diminishing his normal strength. But the theory might also be made to apply to cases where special exertion is undergone for many days or weeks in succession, in order to complete a work, as in collecting the harvest. Adequate motives may lead to and warrant over work, but, if long continued, it reduces the strength and becomes insupportable ; and the longer it continues the worse it is, the law being somewhat similar to that of periodic labour.

Symbolic Statement of the Theory.

We must represent with accuracy these conditions of labour, and we shall find that there are no less than four quantities concerned. Let us represent these quantities as follows—

$t =$ time, or duration of labour.

$l =$ amount of labour, as meaning the aggregate balance of pain accompanying it, irrespective of the produce.

$x =$ amount of commodity produced.

$u =$ total utility of that commodity.

The amount of commodity produced will be very different in different cases. In any one case the rate of production will be determined by dividing the whole quantity produced by the time of production, provided that the rate of production has been uniform; it will then be $\frac{x}{t}$. But if the rate of production be variable, it can only be determined at any moment by comparing an indefinitely small quantity of produce with the indefinitely small portion of time occupied in its production. Thus the rate of production is properly denoted by $\frac{dx}{dt}$.

Again, the degree of painfulness of labour would be $\frac{l}{t}$ if the degree remained invariable; but as it is highly variable, and, in fact, increases with t, we must again compare small increments, and $\frac{\triangle l}{\triangle t}$, or, at the limit, $\frac{dl}{dt}$ correctly represents the *degree of painfulness of labour*. But we must also take into account the fact, that the utility of commodity is not constant. If a man works regularly twelve hours a day, he will produce more commodity than in ten hours; therefore the final degree of utility of his commodity, whether he consume it himself or exchange it, will not be quite so high as when he produced less. This degree of utility is denoted, as before, by $\frac{du}{dx}$, the ratio of the increment of utility to the increment of commodity.

The amount of reward of labour can now be expressed; for it is $\frac{dx}{dt} \cdot \frac{du}{dx}$; that is, it depends upon the compound ratio of the commodity produced to the time, and the utility to the amount of produce. For instance, the last two hours of work in the day may give less reward, both because less produce is then created, and because that produce is less necessary and useful to one who makes enough to support himself in the other ten hours.

We can now readily define the length of time which will be naturally selected as the best term of labour. A free labourer endures the irksomeness of work because the pleasure he receives, or the pain he wards off by means of t e produce, exceeds the pain of exertion. When labour itself is a worse evil than what it saves him from, there can be no motive for further

exertion, and he ceases. Therefore he will cease
to labour just at that point when the pain
exactly equals for a moment the corresponding
pleasure acquired; and we thus have t defined
by the equation

$$\frac{dl}{dt} = \frac{dx}{dt} \cdot \frac{du}{dx}.$$

In this, as in the other questions of Economy,
all depends upon the final increments; and we
have expressed in the above formula *the final
equivalence of labour and utility.* A man must
be regarded as earning all through his hours of
labour an excess of utility; what he produces
must be considered not merely the exact equivalent of the labour he gives for it, for it would
be, in that case, a matter of indifference whether
he laboured or not. As long as he gains, he
labours, and when he ceases to gain, he ceases
to labour.

In many cases, as for instance in machine
labour, the rate of production is uniform, and
by choice of suitable units may be made equal
to unity; the result may then be put more
simply in this way. Labour may be considered
as expended in successive small quantities,
Δl, each lasting, for instance, for a quarter of
an hour; the corresponding benefit derived

from the labour will then be denoted by $\triangle u$. Now, so long as $\triangle u$ exceeds in amount of pleasure the negative quantity or pain of $\triangle l$, there will be a gain inducing to continued labour. Were $\triangle u$ to fall below $\triangle l$, there would positively be more harm than good in labouring; therefore, the boundary between labour and inactivity will be defined by the exact equality of $\triangle u$ and $\triangle l$, or, at the limit between

$$\frac{du}{dx} \text{ and } \frac{dl}{dx};$$

and we have the equation

$$\frac{du}{dx} = \frac{dl}{dx}.$$

Balance between Need and Labour.

In considering this Theory of Labour, an interesting question presents itself. Supposing that circumstances alter the relation of produce to labour, what effect will this have upon the amount of labour which will be exerted? There are two effects to be considered. When labour produces more commodity, there is more reward, and therefore more inducement to labour. If a workman can earn ninepence an hour instead of sixpence, may he not be induced to extend his hours of labour by this increased result? This would doubtless be the case were it not that the very fact of getting half as much more than he did before, lowers the utility to him of any further addition. By the produce of the same number of hours he can satisfy his desires to a higher point; and if the irksomeness of labour has reached at all a high point, he may gain more pleasure by relaxing that labour than by consuming more products. The question thus evidently depends upon the direction in which the balance between the utility of further commodity and the painfulness of labour turns.

In our ignorance of the exact character of the functions either of utility or of labour, it will be impossible to decide this question in an *à priori* manner; but there are a few facts which indicate in which direction the balance does usually turn. Statements are given by Mr. Porter, in his 'Progress of the Nation [e],' which show that when a sudden rise took place in the prices of provisions in the early part of this century, workmen increased their hours of labour, or, as it is said, worked double time if they could obtain adequate employment. Now, a rise in the price of food is really the same as

[e] Edition of 1847, pp. 454, 455.

a decrease of the produce of labour, since less of the necessaries of life can be acquired. We may conclude, then, that English labourers enjoying little more than the necessaries of life, will work harder the less the produce; or, which is the same, will work less hard as the produce increases.

Evidence to the same effect is found in the general tendency to reduce the hours of labour at the present day, owing to the improved real wages now enjoyed by those employed in mills and factories. Artisans, mill-hands, and others generally, seem to prefer greater ease to greater wealth, thus proving that the degree of utility varies more rapidly than the degree of painfulness of labour. The same rule seems to hold throughout the mercantile employments. The richer a man becomes, the less does he devote himself to the business. A successful merchant is generally willing to give a considerable share of his profits to a partner, or a staff of managers and clerks, rather than bear the constant labour of superintendence himself. There is also a general tendency to reduce the hours of labour in mercantile offices, due to increased comfort and opulence.

But there are many exceptions to this rule

furnished by those learned professions where the work is of a more interesting and exciting character. A successful solicitor, barrister, or physician generally labours more severely as his success increases. This result may partly arise from the fact that the work is not easily capable of being refused or performed by deputy. But the case of an eminent architect or engineer is one where the work is to a great extent done by employees, and where yet the most successful man endures the most labour, or rather is most constantly at work. This indicates that the irksomeness of the labour does not increase so as to pass beyond the degree of utility of the increasing reward.

It is evident that questions of this kind will depend greatly upon the character of the race. Persons of an energetic disposition feel labour less painful than they otherwise would, and, if they happen to be endowed with various and acute sensibilities, their desire of further acquisition never ceases. A man of lower race, a negro for instance, enjoys possession less, and loathes labour more; his exertions, therefore, soon stop. A poor savage would be content to gather the almost gratuitous fruits of nature, if they were sufficient to give sustenance; it

N

is only physical want which drives him to exertion.   The rich man in modern society is supplied apparently with all he can desire, and yet he often labours unceasingly for more. Bishop Berkeley, in his 'Querist f,' has very well asked, 'Whether the creating of wants be not the likeliest way to produce industry in a people?   And whether, if our (Irish) peasants were accustomed to eat beef and wear shoes, they would not be more industrious?'

Distribution of Labour.

We now come to consider the conditions which will regulate the comparative amount of different commodities produced in a country. Theoretically speaking, we might regard each person as capable of producing various commodities, and dividing his labour according to certain rules between the different employments; it would not be impossible, too, to mention cases where such division does take place.   But the result of commerce and the division of labour is to make every man find his advantage in performing one trade only; and I give the formulæ as they would apply to an individual, only because they are identical in form with those which apply to a whole nation.

f Query No. 20.

Suppose that an individual is capable of producing three kinds of commodity. His sole object, of course, is to produce the greatest amount of utility; but this will depend partly upon the comparative degrees of utility of the commodities, and partly on his comparative facilities for producing them. Let x, y, z be the respective quantities of the commodities already produced, and suppose that he is about to apply more labour; on which commodity shall he spend the next increment of labour?— Plainly, on that which will yield most utility. Now, if one increment of labour, $\triangle l$, will yield the increments of commodity $\triangle x$, $\triangle y$, $\triangle z$, the ratios of produce to labour—

$$\frac{\triangle x}{\triangle l}, \quad \frac{\triangle y}{\triangle l}, \quad \frac{\triangle z}{\triangle l}$$

will be one element in the problem. But to obtain the comparative utility of these increments, we must multiply by

$$\frac{\triangle u_1}{\triangle x}, \quad \frac{\triangle u_2}{\triangle y}, \quad \frac{\triangle u_3}{\triangle z}.$$

For instance,

$$\frac{\triangle u_1}{\triangle x} \cdot \frac{\triangle x}{\triangle l_1}$$

expresses the amount of utility which can be obtained by producing a little more of the first commodity; if this be greater than the same expression for the other commodities, it would evidently be best to make the first commodity until it ceased to yield any excess of utility. When the labour is finally distributed, we ought to have the increments of utility from each employment equal, and at the limit we have the equations——

$$\frac{du_1}{dx} \cdot \frac{dx}{dl_1} = \frac{du_2}{dy} \cdot \frac{dy}{dl_2} = \frac{du_3}{dz} \cdot \frac{dz}{dl_3}.$$

When these equations hold, there can be no motive for altering or regretting the distribution of labour, and the utility produced is at its maximum.

There are in this problem three unknown quantities, l_1, l_2, l_3, the three portions of labour appropriated to the three commodities. To determine them, we require one other equation in addition to the above. If we put

$$l = l_1 + l_2 + l_3,$$

we have still an unknown quantity to determine, namely, l; but the principles of labour (see pp. 170–4) now give us an equation. Labour will be carried on until the increment of utility from any of the employments just balances the increment of pain.

Relation of the Theories of Labour and Exchange.

It may tend to give the reader confidence in the preceding theories when he finds that they lead directly to the well-known and almost self-evident law, that articles which can be produced in greater or less quantity exchange in proportion to their cost of production. The ratio of exchange of commodities will, as a fact, conform in the long run to the ratio of production.

To simplify our expressions, let us substitute for the ratio of production $\left(\dfrac{dx}{dl}\right)$ the symbol ϖ. Then ϖ_1, ϖ_2, ϖ_3 express the relative quantities of the different commodities produced by an increment of labour, and we have the following equations, identical with those on the last page.

$$\phi x \cdot \varpi_1 = \psi y \cdot \varpi_2 = \chi z \cdot \varpi_3.$$

Let us suppose that the person to whom they apply is in a position to exchange with other persons. The conditions of production will now, in all probability, be modified. For x the quantity of our commodity may perhaps be increased to $x + x_1$, and y diminished to $y - y_1$, by an exchange of the quantities x_1 and y_1. If this be so, we shall, as shown in the Theory of Exchange, have the equation

$$\frac{\phi\,(x + x_1)}{\psi\,(y - y_1)} = \frac{y_1}{x_1}.$$

Our equation of production will now be modified, and become

$$\phi\,(x + x_1)\,.\,\varpi_1 = \psi\,(y - y_1)\,\varpi_2\,;$$

or

$$\frac{\phi\,(x + x_1)}{\psi\,(y - y_1)} = \frac{\varpi_2}{\varpi_1}.$$

But this equation has its first member identical with the first member of the equation of exchange given above, so that we may at once deduce the all-important equation

$$\frac{\varpi_2}{\varpi_1} = \frac{y_1}{x_1}.$$

The reader will remember that ϖ expresses the ratio of produce to labour; thus we have proved that commodities will exchange in any market in the ratio of the quantities produced by the same quantity of labour. But as the increment of labour considered is always the final one, our equation also expresses the truth, that *articles will exchange in quantities inversely as the cost of production of the most costly portions, i. e. the last portions added.* This last point will prove of great importance in the theory of Rent.

Let it be observed that, in uniting the theories of exchange and production, a complicated double adjustment takes place in the quantities of commodity involved. Each party adjusts not only its consumption of articles in accordance with their ratio of exchange, but it also adjusts its production of them. The ratio of exchange governs the production as much as the production governs the ratio of exchange. For instance, since the Corn Laws have been abolished in England, the effect has been, not to destroy the culture of wheat, but to lessen it. The land less suitable to the growth of wheat has been turned to grazing or other purposes more profitable comparatively speaking. Similarly the importation of hops or eggs or any other article of food does not even reduce the quantity raised here, but prevents the necessity for resorting to more expensive modes of gaining a supply. It is not easy to express in words how the ratios of exchange are finally determined. They depend upon a general balance of producing power and of demand as measured by the final ratio of utility. Every additional supply tends to lower the degree of utility; but whether that supply will be forthcoming from any country depends upon its comparative powers of producing different commodities.

Any very small tract of country cannot appreciably affect the comparative supply of commodities : it must therefore adjust its productions in accordance with the general state of the market.   The county of Bedford, for instance, would not appreciably affect the markets for corn, cheese, or cattle, whether it devoted every acre to .corn or to grazing.   Therefore the agriculture of Bedfordshire will have to be adapted to circumstances, and each field will be employed for arable or grazing land according as prevailing prices render one employment or the other more profitable.   But any large country will affect the markets as well as be affected.   If the whole habitable surface of Australia, instead of producing wool, could be turned to the . cultivation of wine, the wool market would rise, and the wine market fall. If the Southern States of America abandoned cotton in favour of sugar, there would be a revolution in these markets.   It would be inevitable for Australia to return to wool and the American States to cotton.   These are illustrations of the reciprocal relation of exchange and production.

Various Cases of the Theory.

As we have now reached the principal question in Political Economy, it will be well to consider the meaning and results of our equations in some detail.

It will, in the first place, be apparent, that the absolute facility of producing commodities will not determine the character and amount of trade. The ratio of exchange $\frac{y_1}{x_1}$ is not determined by ϖ_1, nor by ϖ_2 separately, but by their comparative magnitude. If the producing power of a country were doubled, no direct effect would be produced upon the terms of its commerce if the increase were equal in all branches of its production. This is a point of great importance, which was correctly conceived by Ricardo, and has been fully explained by Mr. Mill.

But though there is no such direct effect, it may happen that there will be an indirect effect through the variation in the degree of utility of different articles. When an increased amount of every commodity can be produced, it is not likely that the increase will be equally desired

in each branch of consumption.   Hence the
degree of utility will fall in some cases more
than others.   An alteration of the ratios of exchange must result, and the production of the
less needed commodities will not be extended so
much as in the case of the more needed ones.
We might find in such instances new proofs
that value depends not upon labour but upon
the degree of utility.

It will also be apparent, that nations possessing exactly similar powers of production cannot
gain by mutual commerce, and consequently
will not have any such commerce, however
free from artificial restrictions.   We get this
result as follows—Let ϖ_1 ϖ_2 be the final ratios
of production in one country, and μ_1 μ_2 in a
second; then, if the conditions of production
are exactly similar, we have

$$\frac{\varpi_2}{\varpi_1} = \frac{\mu_2}{\mu_1}.$$

But when a country does not trade at all, its
labour and consumption is distributed according to the condition

$$\frac{\phi x}{\psi y} = \frac{\varpi_2}{\varpi_1}.$$

Now, from these equations, it follows necessarily, that

$$\frac{\phi\, x}{\psi\, y} = \frac{\mu_2}{\mu_1};$$

that is to say, the production and consumption already conform to the conditions of production of the second country, and will not undergo any alteration when trade with this country becomes possible.

This is the doctrine usually stated in works on Political Economy, and for which there are good grounds. But I do not think the statement will hold true if the conditions of consumption be very different in two countries. There might be two countries exactly similar in regard to their powers of producing beef and corn, and if their habits of consumption were also exactly similar, there would be no trade in these articles. But suppose that the first country consumed proportionally more beef, and the second more corn; then, if there were no trade, the powers of the soil would be differently taxed, and different ratios of exchange would prevail. Freedom of trade would cause an interchange of corn for beef. Thus I should conclude, that it is only where the habits of consumption, as well as the powers of production, are alike, that trade brings no advantage.

The general effect of foreign commerce is to

disturb, to the advantage of a country, the
mode in which it distributes its labour.   Ex-
cluding from view the cost of carriage, and the
other expenses of commerce, we must always
have true

$$\frac{\varpi_2}{\varpi_1} = \frac{y_1}{x_1} = \frac{\mu_2}{\mu_1}.$$

If, then, ϖ_2 was originally in less proportion
to ϖ_1 than is in accordance with these equations, some labour will be transferred from the
production of y to that of x until, by the increased magnitude of ϖ_2, and the lessened
magnitude of ϖ_1, equality is brought about.

As in the theory of exchange, so in the
theory of production, any of the equations may
fail, and the meaning is capable of interpretation.   Thus, if the equation

$$\frac{\varpi_2}{\varpi_1} = \frac{y_1}{x_1}$$

cannot be established, it is impossible that the
production of both commodities, y and x, can
go on.   One of them will be produced at an
expenditure of labour constantly out of proportion to that at which it may be had by exchange.
If we could not, for instance, import oranges
from abroad, part of the labour of the country
would probably be diverted from its present

employment to raise them, but the cost of production would be always above that of getting them indirectly by exchange, so that free trade necessarily destroys such a wasteful branch of industry. It is on this principle that we import the whole of our wines, teas, sugar, coffee, spices, and many other articles from abroad.

The ratio of exchange of any two commodities will be determined by a kind of struggle between the conditions of consumption and production ; but here again failure of the equations may take place. In the all-important equations

$$\frac{\phi\,(x + x_1)}{\psi\,(y - y_1)} = \frac{\varpi_2}{\varpi_1} = \frac{y_1}{x_1},$$

ϖ_2 expresses the ease with which we may make additions to y. If we find any means, by machinery or otherwise, of increasing y without limit, and with the same ease as before, we must, in all probability, alter the ratio of exchange $\frac{y_1}{x_1}$ in a corresponding degree. But if we could imagine the existence of a large population, within reach of the supposed country, whose desire to consume the quantity y_1 never decreased, however large was the quantity available, then we should never have $\frac{y_1}{x_1}$ equal to

$\frac{\varpi_2}{\varpi_1}$, and the producers of y would make large gains of the nature of rent.

Of Over-production.

The theory of the distribution of labour enables us to perceive clearly the meaning of *over-production* in trade. Early writers on Economy were always in fear of a supposed *glut*, arising from the powers of production surpassing the needs of consumers, so that industry would be stopped, employment fail, and all but the rich would be starved by the superfluity of commodities. The doctrine is evidently absurd and self-contradictory. As the acquirement of suitable commodities is the whole purpose of industry and trade, the greater the supplies obtained the more perfectly industry fulfils its purpose. A universal glut is really the maximising of the results of labour, which is the problem of the economist. But the supplies must be *suitable*—that is, they must be in proportion to the needs of the population. Over-production is not possible in all branches of industry at once, but it is possible in some as compared with others. If, by a miscalculation, too much labour is spent in producing one commodity, say silk goods, our equations will not hold true. People will be more satiated with silk goods than cotton, woollen or other goods. They will refuse, therefore, to purchase them at ratios of exchange corresponding to the labour expended. The producers will thus receive in exchange goods of less utility than they might have acquired by a better distribution of their labour.

In extending industry, therefore, we must be careful to extend it proportionally to all the requirements of the population. The more we can lower the degree of utility of all goods by satiating the desires of the purchasers the better; but we must lower the degrees of utility of different goods in a corresponding manner, otherwise there is an apparent glut and a real loss of labour.

Limits to the Intensity of Labour.

I have mentioned (p. 165) that labour may vary either in duration or intensity, but have yet paid little attention to the latter circumstance. We may approximately measure the intensity of labour by the amount of physical force undergone in a certain time, although it is the pain attending that exertion of force which is the all-important element in Economy. Interesting laws have been or may be detected connecting the amount of work done with the intensity of labour.   Even where these laws have not been ascertained, long experience has led men, by a sort of unconscious reasoning, to select that rate of work which is most advantageous.

Let us take such a simple kind of work as digging.   A spade may be made of any size, and if the same number of strokes be made in the hour, the exertion requisite will vary nearly as the cube of the length of the blade.   If the spade be small, the fatigue will be slight, but the work done will also be slight.   A very large spade, on the other hand, will do a great quantity of work at each stroke, but the fatigue will be so great that the labourer cannot long continue at his work.   Accordingly, a certain medium-sized spade is adopted, which does not overtax a labourer and prevent him doing a full day's work, but enables him to accomplish as much as possible.   The size of a spade should depend partly upon the tenacity and weight of the material, and partly upon the strength of the labourer.   It may be observed that, in excavating stiff clay, navvies use a small strong spade; for ordinary garden purposes a larger spade is employed; for shovelling loose sand or coals a broad capacious shovel is used; and a still larger instrument is employed for removing corn, malt, or any loose powder.

In most cases of muscular exertion the weight of the body or of some limb is of great importance. If a man be employed to carry a single letter, he really moves a weight of say a hundred and sixty pounds for the purpose of conveying a letter weighing perhaps half an ounce. There will be no appreciable increase of labour if he carries two letters or twenty letters, so that his efficiency will be multiplied twenty times. A hundred letters would probably prove a slight burden, but there would still be a vast gain in the work done. It is obvious, however, that we might go on loading a postman with letters until the fatigue became excessive; the maximum useful result would be obtained with the largest load which does not severely fatigue the man, and trial soon decides the weight with considerable accuracy.

The most favourable load for a porter was investigated by Coulomb, and he found that most work could be done by a man walking up-

o

stairs without any load, and raising his burden by means of his own weight in descending. A man could thus raise four times as much in a day as by carrying bags on his back with the most favourable load. This great difference doubtless arises from the muscles being perfectly adapted to raising the human body, whereas any additional weight throws irregular or undue stress upon them. Mr. Babbage, also, in his admirable 'Economy of Manufactures' (p. 30), has remarked on this subject, and has pointed out that the weight of some limb of the body is an element in all calculations of human labour.

It occurred to me, some time since, that this was a subject admitting of interesting inquiry, and I tried to determine, by several series of experiments, the relation between the amount of work done by certain muscles and the rate of fatigue. One series consisted in holding weights varying from one pound to eighteen pounds in the hand while the arm was stretched out at its full length. The trials were two hundred and thirty-eight in number, and were made at intervals of at least one hour, so that the fatigue of one trial should not derange the next. The average number of seconds during which each weight could be sustained was found to be as follows—

Weight in pounds	18	14	10	7	4	2	1
Time in seconds ..	15	32	60	87	148	219	321.

If the arm had been thus employed in any kind of useful work, we should have estimated the useful effect by the product of the weight sustained and the time. The results would be as follows, in pound-seconds—

Weight	18	14	10	7	4	2	1
Useful effect	266	455	603	612	592	438	321.

The maximum of useful effect would here appear to be about seven pounds, which is about the weight usually chosen for dumb-bells or other gymnastic exercises. Details of the other series of experiments are described in an article in *Nature* (30th June, 1870, vol. ii. p. 158).

I undertook these experiments as a mere illustration of the mode in which some of the laws forming the physical basis of Political Economy might be ascertained. I was unaware that Professor S. Haughton had already, by experiment, arrived at a theory of muscular action, communicated to the Royal Society in 1862. I was gratified to find that my entirely independent results proved to be in striking

<u>agreement with his principles</u>, as was pointed out by Professor Haughton in two articles in *Nature* g.

I am not aware that any exact experiments upon walking or marching have been made, but, as Professor Haughton has remarked to me, they might easily be carried out in the movements of an army. It would only be necessary, on each march which is carried up to the limits of endurance, to register the time and distance passed over. Had we a determination of the exact relations of time, space, and fatigue, it would be possible to solve many interesting problems. For instance, if one person has to overtake another, what should be their comparative rates of walking? Assuming the fatigue to increase as the square of the velocity multiplied by the time, I easily obtained an exact solution, showing that the total fatigue would be least when the person goes twice as quickly as him whom he wishes to overtake.

In different cases of muscular exertion we shall find different problems to solve. The most advantageous rate of marching will greatly depend upon whether the loss of time or the fatigue is the most important. Great rapidity,

g Vol. ii. p. 324 ; vol. iii. p. 289.

for instance four or four and a half miles an hour, would soon occasion enormous fatigue, and could only be resorted to when there was great urgency. The distance passed over would bear a much higher ratio to the fatigue at the rate of three or two and a half miles an hour. But if the speed were still further reduced, a loss of strength would again arise, owing to that expended in merely sustaining the body as distinguished from that of moving it forward.

The Political Economy of Labour will constantly involve questions of this kind. When a work has to be completed in a brief space of time, workmen may be incited by unusual reward to do far more than their usual amount of work; but so high a rate would not be profitable in other circumstances. The fatigue always rapidly increases when the speed of work passes a certain point, so that the extra result is far more costly in reality. In a regular and constant employment the greatest result will always be gained by such a rate as allows a workman each day, or each week at the most, to recover all fatigue and recommence with an undiminished store of energy.

CHAPTER VI.

THEORY OF RENT.

Accepted Opinions concerning Rent.

THE general correctness of the views put
forth in preceding chapters derives great probability from their close resemblance to the
Theory of Rent, as it has been accepted by
English writers for nearly a century. It has
not been usual to state this theory in mathematical symbols, and clumsy arithmetical illustrations have been employed instead ; but it is
easy to show that the fluxional calculus is the
branch of mathematics which most correctly
applies to the subject.

The Theory of Rent was first discovered and
clearly stated by James Anderson in a tract
published in 1777, and called 'An Inquiry into
the Nature of the Corn Laws, with a view to
the Corn Bill proposed for Scotland.' An ex-

tract from this work may be found in Mr. Mac-
Culloch's edition of the 'Wealth of Nations,'
p. 453, giving a most clear explanation of the
effect of the various fertility of land, and showing that it is not the rent of land which determines the price of its produce, but the price of
the produce which determines the rent of the
land. The following passage must be given in
Anderson's own words [a] :——

'. . . In every country there is a variety of
soils, differing considerably from one another in
point of fertility. These we shall at present
suppose arranged into different classes, which
we shall denote by the letters A, B, C, D, E, F,
&c., the class A comprehending the soils of the
greatest fertility, and the other letters expressing different classes of soils, gradually decreasing in fertility as you recede from the first.
Now, as the expense of cultivating the least
fertile soil is as great, or greater than that of
the most fertile field, it n cessarily follows, that
if an equal quantity of corn, the produce of
each field, can be sold at the same price, the
profit on cultivating the most fertile soil must
be much greater than that of cultivating the
others; and as this continues to decrease as

[a] ' Inquiry,' &c. p. 45 ; *note.*

the sterility increases, it must at length happen, that the expense of cultivating some of
the inferior soils will equal the value of the
whole produce.'

The theory really rests upon the principle
already enumerated (p. 91), that for the same
commodity in the same market there can only
be one price or ratio of exchange. Hence, if
different qualities of land yield different amounts
of produce to the same labour, there must be
an excess of profit in some over others. There
will be some land which will not yield the ordinary wages of labour, and which will, therefore,
not be taken into cultivation, or if, by mistake,
it is cultivated, will be abandoned. Some land
will just pay the ordinary wages ; better land
will yield an excess, so that the possession of
such land will become a matter of competition,
and the owner will be able to exact as rent
from the cultivators the whole excess above
what is sufficient to pay the ordinary wages of
labour.

There is a secondary origin for rent in the
fact, that if more or less labour and capital
be applied to the same portion of land, the
produce will not increase proportionally to the
amount of labour. It is quite impossible that

we could go on constantly increasing the yield of one farm without limit, otherwise we might feed the whole country upon a single farm. Yet there is no definite limit; for, by better and better culture we may always seem able to raise a little more. But the last increment of produce will come to bear a smaller and smaller ratio to the labour required to produce it, so that it soon becomes, in the case of all land, undesirable to apply more labour.

Mr. MacCulloch has given, in his edition of Adam Smith's 'Wealth of Nations b,' a supplementary note, in which he explains, with the utmost clearness and scientific accuracy, the nature of the theory. This note contains by far the best statement of the theory, as it seems to me, and I will therefore quote his recapitulation of the principles which he establishes.

'1. That if the produce of land could always be increased in proportion to the outlay on it, there would be no such thing as rent.

'2. That the produce of land cannot, at an average, be increased in proportion to the outlay, but may be indefinitely increased in a less proportion.

b New edition, 1839, p. 444.

'3. That the least productive portion of the outlay, which, speaking generally, is the last, must yield the ordinary profits of stock. And

'4. That all which the other portions yield more than this, being above ordinary profits, is rent.'

A most satisfactory account of the theory is also given in Mr. James Mill's 'Elements of Political Economy,' a work which I never read without admiration at its brief, clear, and powerful style. Mr. Mill uses constantly the expression *dose of capital*. 'The time comes,' he says, 'at which it is necessary either to have recourse to land of the second quality, or to apply a second dose of capital less productively upon land of the first quality.' He evidently means by a *dose of capital* a little more capital, and though the name is peculiar, the meaning is that of an *increment of capital*. The number of doses or increments mentioned is only three, but this is clearly to avoid prolixity of explanation. There is no reason why we should not consider the whole capital divided into many more doses. The same general law which makes the second dose less productive than the first, will make a hundredth dose,

speaking generally, less productive than the preceding ninety-ninth dose. Theoretically speaking,
there is no need or possibility of stopping at any
limit. A mathematical law is always continuous, so that the *doses* considered are indefinitely
small or indefinitely numerous. I consider, then,
that Mr. James Mill's mode of expression is
exactly equivalent to that which I have adopted
in earlier parts of this book. As mathematicians have invented a precise and fully recognised mode of expressing *doses or increments*, I
know not why we should exclude language from
Political Economy which is found convenient in
all other sciences.

The following are Mr. James Mill's general
conclusions as to the nature of Rent [c].

' In applying capital, either to lands of various
degrees of fertility, or in successive doses to the
same land, some portions of the capital so employed are attended with a greater produce,
some with a less. That which yields the least,
yields all that is necessary for re-imbursing and
rewarding the capitalist. The capitalist will
receive no more than this remuneration for any
portion of the capital which he employs, because the competition of others will prevent

[c] ' Elements,' p. 17.

him.   All that is yielded above this remuneration the landlord will be able to appropriate. Rent, therefore, is the difference between the return yielded to that portion of the capital which is employed upon the land with the least effect, and that which is yielded to all the other portions employed upon it with a greater effect.'

Symbolic Statement of the Theory.

The accepted Theory of Rent, as given above, needs little or no alteration to adapt it to expression in mathematical symbols.   For doses or increments of capital I shall substitute increments of labour, partly because the functions of capital remain to be considered in the next chapter, and partly because Mr. James Mill, Mr. J. S. Mill, and Mr. MacCulloch hold the application of capital to be synonymous with the application of labour.   It is implied in Mr. James Mill's statement (p. 13); it is expressly stated in Mr. J. S. Mill's 'First Fundamental Proposition concerning the Nature of Capital [d];' and Mr. MacCulloch adds a foot-note [e] to make it clear, that as all capital was originally pro-

[d] Book i. chapter 5, § 1.   [e] 'Wealth of Nations,' p. 445.

duced by labour, the application of additional capital is the application of additional labour. 'Either the one phrase or the other may be used indiscriminately.'

I shall suppose that a certain labourer, or, what comes to exactly the same, a body of labourers, expend labour on several different pieces of ground. On what principle will they distribute their labour between the several pieces? Let us imagine that a certain amount has been spent upon each, and that another small portion, $\triangle l$, is going to be applied. Let there be three pieces of land, and let $\triangle x_1$, $\triangle x_2$, $\triangle x_3$ be the increments of produce to be expected from the pieces respectively. They will naturally apply the labour to the land which yields the greatest result. So long as there is any advantage in one use of labour over another, the most advantageous will certainly be adopted. Therefore, when they are perfectly satisfied with the distribution made, the increment of produce to the same labour will be equal in each case; or we have

$$\triangle x_1 = \triangle x_2 = \triangle x_3.$$

To attain scientific accuracy, we must decrease the increments indefinitely, and then we obtain the equations—

$$\frac{dx_1}{dl_1} = \frac{dx_2}{dl_2} = \frac{dx_3}{dl_3}.$$

Now $\frac{dx}{dl}$ represents the ratio of produce, or the productiveness of labour, as regards the last increment of labour applied. We may say, then, that whenever a labourer or body of labourers distribute their labour over several pieces of land with perfect economy, the *final ratios of produce to labour will be equal.*

We may now take into account the general law, that when more and more labour is applied to the same piece of land, the produce ultimately does not increase proportionally to the labour. This means that the function $\frac{dx}{dl}$ diminishes without limit after x has passed a certain quantity. The whole produce of a piece of land is x, the whole labour spent upon it is l; and x varies in some way as l varies, never decreasing when l increases. We may say, then, that x is a function of l; let us call it Pl. When a little more labour is expended, the increment of produce dx is dPl, and $\frac{dPl}{dl}$ is the final rate of production, the same as was previously denoted by $\frac{dx}{dl}$.

In the Theory of Labour it was shown that no increment of labour would be expended unless there was sufficient recompense in the produce, but that labour would be expended up to the point at which the increment of utility exactly equals the increment of pain incurred in acquiring it. Here we find an exact definition of the amount of labour which will be profitably applied.

It was also shown that the last increment of labour is the most painful, so that if a person is recompensed for the last increment of labour which he applies to land by the rate of production $\frac{dx}{dl}$, it follows that all the labour he applies might be recompensed sufficiently at the same rate. The whole labour is l, so that if the recompense be equal over the whole, the result would be $l . \frac{dx}{dl}$. Consequently, he obtains more than the necessary return to labour by the amount

$$Pl - l . \frac{dx}{dl} ;$$

or, as we may write it,

$$Pl - l . P'l,$$

in which $P'l$ is the differential coefficient of Pl,

or the final rate of production. This expression represents the advantage he derives from the possession of land in affording him more profit than other methods of employing his labour. It is therefore the rent which he would ask before yielding it up to another person, or equally the rent which he would be able and willing to pay if hiring it from another.

The same considerations apply to every piece of land cultivated. When the same person or body of labourers cultivate several pieces, Pl will be the same quantity in each case, but the quantities of labour, and possibly the functions of labour, will be different. Thus with two pieces of land the rent may be represented as

$$P_1 l_1 + P_2 l_2 - (l_1 + l_2) P_1' l_1$$

or, speaking generally of any number of pieces, it is the sum of the quantities of the form Pl, *minus* the sum of the quantities $l.Pl.$.

Illustration of the Theory.

It is very easy to illustrate the Theory of Rent by diagrams. For, let distances along the line *ox* denote quantities of labour, and let the curve *apc* represent the variation of the rate of production, so that the area of the curve will

production, so that the area of the curve will
be the measure of the produce.   Thus when
labour has been applied to the amount *om*, the
produce will correspond to the area *apmo*.   Let
a small new increment of labour, *mm'*, be applied, and suppose the rate of production equal
over the whole of the increment.   Then the

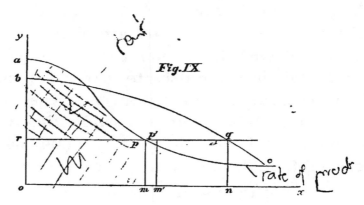

Fig. IX

small parallelogram, *pp'm'm* will be the produce.
This will be proportional in quantity to *pm*, so
that the height of any point of the curve per-
pendicularly above a point of the line *ox* represents the rate of production at that point in
the application of labour.

· If we further suppose that the labourer considers his labour, *mm'*, repaid by the produce
pm', there is no reason why any other part of
his labour should not be repaid at the same

P

rate.   Drawing, then, a horizontal line, *rpq*, through the point *p*, his whole labour, *om*, will be repaid by the produce represented by the area *orpm*.   Consequently, the overlying area, *rap*, is the excess of produce which can be exacted from him as rent, if he be not himself the owner of the land.

Imagining the same person to cultivate another piece of land, we might take the curve, *bqc*, to represent its productiveness.   The same rate of production will repay the labourer in this case as in the last, so that the intersection of the same horizontal line, *rpq* with the curve, will determine the final point of labour, *n*. The area, *rn*, will be the measure of the sufficient recompense to the whole labour, *on*, spent upon the land; and the excess of produce or rent will be the area *rbq*.   In a similar manner, any number of pieces of land might be considered.   The figure might have been drawn so that the curves would rise on leaving the initial line *oy*, indicating that a very little labour will have a poor rate of production; and that a certain amount of labour is requisite to develop the fertility of the soil. This may often or always be the case, as a considerable quantity of labour is generally requisite in first bringing land into cultivation, or merely keeping it in a fit state for use. The laws of rent depend on the undoubted principle, that the curves always *ultimately* decline towards the base line *ox*, that is the final rate of production always *ultimately* sinks towards zero.

CHAPTER VII.

THEORY OF CAPITAL.

On the True Nature and Definition of Capital.

In considering the nature and principles of Capital, we enter a distinct branch of our subject. There is no close or necessary connection between the employment of capital and the processes of exchange. Both by capital and exchange we are enabled vastly to increase the sum of utility which we enjoy; but it is just conceivable that we might have the advantages of capital without those of exchange. An isolated man like Alexander Selkirk, or an isolated family, might feel the great benefit of a stock of provisions, tools, and other means of facilitating industry, although cut off from traffic with any others of the race. Political Economy, then, is not solely the science of Exchange- or -Value-:—it is also the science of Capital.——

The views which I shall endeavour to establish on this subject are, I believe, in fundamental agreement with those adopted by Mr. Ricardo; but I shall try to put the Theory of Capital in a more simple and consistent manner than has been the case with some later economists. We are told, with perfect truth, that capital consists of wealth employed to facilitate production ; but when economists proceed to enumerate the articles of wealth constituting capital, they obscure the subject. 'The capital of a country,' says MacCulloch [a], 'consists of those portions of the produce of industry existing in it, which may be directly employed either to support human beings, or to facilitate production.' Professor Fawcett again says [b]: 'Capital is not confined to the food which feeds the labourers; but includes machinery, buildings, and in fact, every product due to man's labour which can be applied to assist his industry;

[a] ' Principles of Political Economy,' p. 100.
[b] ' Manual of Political Economy,' second edition, p. 47.

but capital which is in the form of food does not perform its functions in the same way as capital that is in the form of machinery : the one is termed circulating capital, the other fixed capital.'

The notion of capital assumes a new degree of simplicity as soon as we recognise that what has been called a part is really the whole. Capital, as I shall treat it, consists merely in the *aggregate of those commodities which are required for sustaining labourers of any kind or class engaged in work.* A stock of food is the main element of capital; but supplies of clothes, furniture, and all the other articles in common daily use are also necessary parts of capital. The *current means of sustenance constitute capital in its free or uninvested form.* The single and all-important purpose of capital is to enable the labourer to await the result of any long-lasting work,—to put an interval between the beginning and the end of an enterprise.

Not only can we, by the aid of capital, erect large works which would otherwise have been impossible, but the production of articles which would have been very costly in labour may be rendered far more easy. Capital enables us to make a great outlay in providing tools, machines, or other preliminary works, which have for their sole object the production of some other commodity, but which will greatly facilitate production when we enter upon it.

Several economists have clearly perceived that the time elapsing between the beginning and end of a work is the difficulty which capital assists us to surmount. Thus one writer has said—'If the man who subsists on animals cannot make sure of his prey in less than a day, he cannot have less than a whole day's subsistence in advance. If hunting excursions are undertaken which occupy a week or a month, subsistence for several days may be required. It is evident, when men come to live upon those productions which their labour raises from the soil, and which can be brought to maturity only once in the year, that subsistence for a whole year must be laid up in advance.'

Much more recently, Professor Hearn has said, in his admirable work entitled 'Plutology c,'— 'The first and most obvious mode in which capital directly operates as an auxiliary of industry is to render possible the performance of work which requires for its completion some

c 'Plutology; or the Theory of Efforts to Satisfy Human Wants,' 1864 (Macmillan), p. 139.

considerable time./ In the simplest agricultural operations there is the seed time and the harvest. A vineyard is unproductive for at least three years before it is thoroughly fit for use. In gold mining there is often a long delay, sometimes even of five or six years, before the gold is reached. Such mines could not be worked by poor men unless the storekeepers gave the miners credit, or, in other words, supplied capital for the adventure. But, in addition to this great result, capital also implies other consequences which are hardly less momentous. One of these is the steadiness and continuity that labour thus acquires. A man, when aided by capital, can afford to remain at his work until it is finished, and is not compelled to leave it incomplete while he searches for the necessary means of subsistence. If there were no accumulated fund upon which the labourer could rely, no man could remain for a single day exclusively engaged in any other occupation than those which relate to the supply of his primary wants. Besides these wants, he should also from time to time search for the materials on which he was to work.'

These passages imply, as it seems to me, a clear insight into the nature and purposes of

capital, except that the writers have not with
sufficient boldness followed out the consequences of their notion. If we take a comprehensive view of the subject, it will be seen that
not only the chief, but the sole purpose of capital is as above described. Capital simply allows
us *to expend labour in advance.* Thus, to raise
corn we need to turn over the surface of the
soil. If we proceed straight to the work, and
use the implements with which nature has furnished us—our fingers—we should spend an
enormous amount of painful labour with very
little result. It is far better, therefore, to spend
the first part of our labour in making a spade
or other implement to assist the rest of our
labour. This spade represents so much labour
which has been invested, and so far spent ; but
if it lasts three years, its cost may be considered as repaid gradually during those three
years. This labour, like that of digging, has
for its object the raising of corn, and the only
essential difference is, that it has to precede the
production of corn by a longer interval. The
average period of time for which labour will
remain invested in the spade is half of the three
years. Similarly, if we possess a larger capital,
and expend it in making a plough, which will

last for twenty years, we invest at the beginning a great deal of labour which is only gradually repaid during those twenty years, and which is, on the average, invested for ten years.

It is true that in modern industry we should never find the same man making the spade or plough, and afterwards using the implement. The division of labour enables me, with much advantage, to expend a portion of my capital in purchasing the implement from some one who devotes his attention to the manufacture, and probably expends capital previously in facilitating the work. But this does not alter the principles of the matter. What capital I give for the spade merely replaces what the manufacturer had already invested in the expectation that the spade would be needed. Exactly the same considerations may be applied to much more complicated applications of capital. The ultimate object of all industry engaged with cotton is the production of cotton goods. But the complete process of producing those goods is divided into many parts; and it is necessary to begin the spending of labour a long time before any goods can be finished. In the first place, labour will be required to till the land which is to bear the cotton plants, and probably two years at least will elapse between the time when the ground is first broken and the cotton reaches the mills. A cotton mill, again, if it be efficient at all, must be a very strong and durable structure, and must contain machinery of a very costly character, which can only repay its owner by a long course of use. We might spin and weave cotton goods as in former times, or as it is done in Cashmere, with a very small use of capital; but then the labour required would be enormously greater.

It is far more economical in the end, to spend a vast amount of labour and capital in building a substantial mill and filling it with the best machinery, which will perhaps go on working with unimpaired efficiency for say twenty years. This means that, in addition to the labour spent in superintending the machines at the moment when goods are produced, a great quantity of labour has been spent from one to twenty years in advance, or, on the average, ten years in advance. This expenditure is repaid by an annuity of profit extending over those twenty years.

The interval elapsing between the first exertion of labour and the enjoyment of the result is further increased by any time during which the raw material may lie in warehouses before reaching the machines ; and by the time employed in distributing the goods to retail dealers, and through them to the consumers.   It may even happen that the consumer finds it desirable to keep a certain stock on hand, so that the time when the real object of the goods is fulfilled becomes still further deferred.   During this time, also, capital seems to me to be invested, and only as actual consumption takes place is expenditure repaid by corresponding utility enjoyed.

I would say, then, in the most general manner, that *whatever improvements in the supply of commodities lengthen the average interval between the moment when any labour is exerted and its ultimate result or purpose accomplished, require the use of capital.* And I would add, that this is the sole use of capital. Whenever we overlook the irrelevant complications introduced by the division of labour and the frequency of exchange, all employments of capital resolve themselves into the fact of time elapsing between the beginning and the end of industry.

Quantitative Notions concerning Capital.

One main point which has to be clearly brought before the mind in this subject is the difference between the amount of capital invested and the amount of investment of capital. The first is a quantity of one dimension only— the quantity of capital; the second is a quantity of two dimensions, namely, the quantity of capital, and the length of time during which it remains invested. If one day's labour remains invested for two years, the capital is only that equivalent to one day; but it is locked up twice as long as if there were only one year's investment. Now all questions in which we consider the most advantageous employment of capital turn upon the length of investment quite as much as upon the amount. The same capital will serve for twice as much industry if it be absorbed or invested for only half the time.

The amount of investment of capital will evidently be determined by multiplying each portion of capital invested at any moment by the length of time for which it remains invested. One pound invested for five years gives the same result as five pounds invested for one year, the product being *five pound-years*. Most com-

monly, however, investment proceeds continuously or at intervals, and we must form clear
notions on the subject. Thus, if a workman be
employed during one year on any work, the
result of which is complete, and enjoyed at the
end of that time, the absorption of capital will
be found by multiplying each day's wages by
the days remaining till the end of the year,
and adding all the results together. If the daily
wages be four shillings, then we have

$$4 \times 364 + 4 \times 363 + 4 \times 362 \ldots \ldots + 4 \times 0;$$

or, $4 \times \dfrac{365 \times 364}{2}$, or 265,720 *shilling days*.

We may also represent the investment by a
diagram such as Fig. X. The length along the
line *ox* indicates the duration of investment,

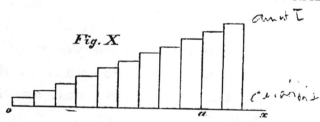

Fig. X

and the height attained at any point, *a*, is the
amount of capital invested. But it is the
whole area of the rectangles up to any point,
a, which measures the amount of investment.
The whole result of continued labour is not

often consumed and enjoyed in a moment ; the result generally lasts. We must then conceive the capital as being progressively uninvested. Let us, for sake of simple illustration, imagine the labour of producing the harvest to be continuously and equally expended between the first of September in one year and the same day in the next. Let the harvest be then completely gathered and its consumption begin, to continue equally during the succeeding twelve months. Then the amount of investment of capital will be represented by the area of an isosceles triangle, as in Fig. XI, the base

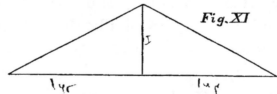

Fig. XI

of which corresponds to two years of duration. Now the area of a triangle is equal to the height multiplied by half the base ; and as the height represents the greatest amount invested, that upon the first of September, when the harvest is gathered ; half the base, or one year, is the *average time of investment of the whole amount.*

In the 37th proposition of the first book of Euclid it is proved that all triangles upon the same base and between the same parallels are equal in area. Hence we may draw the conclusion that, provided capital be invested and uninvested continuously and proportionally to the time, we need only regard the greatest amount invested and the greatest time of investment. Whether it be all invested suddenly, and then gradually withdrawn ; or gradually invested and suddenly withdrawn ; or gradually invested and gradually withdrawn ; the amount of investment will be in every case the greatest amount of capital multiplied by half the time elapsing from the beginning to the complete end of the investment.

Expression for Amount of Investment.

To render our notions of the subject still more exact and general, let us resort to mathematical symbols.

Let $p =$ amount of capital supposed to be invested instantaneously at any moment; let $t =$ time elapsing before its result is enjoyed, also supposed to be instantaneous. Then $p \times t$ is the amount of investment ; and if the investment is repeated, the sum of the quantities of the nature of $p \times t$, or, in the customary mode of expression, Σpt is the total amount of investment. But it will seldom be possible to assign each portion of result to an exactly corresponding portion of the labour. Cotton goods are due to the aggregate industry of those who tilled the ground, grew the cotton, plucked, transported, cleaned, spun, wove, and dyed it; we cannot distinguish the moment when each labourer's work is separately repaid. To avoid this difficulty, we must fix on some moment of time when the whole transaction is closed, all labour upon the ground repaid, the mill and machinery worn out and sold, and the cotton goods consumed. Let t now denote the time elapsing from any moment up to this final moment of closing the accounts. Let p be as before quantities of capital invested, and let q be quantities of capital uninvested by the sale of the products and their enjoyment by the consumer. Thus it will be pretty obvious that the sum of the quantities $p \times t$, less by the sum of the quantities $q \times t$, will be the total investment of capital, or in symbols $\Sigma pt - \Sigma qt$.

Effect of the Duration of Work.

Perhaps the most interesting point in the Theory of Capital is the advantage arising from the rapid performance of work, if it is capable

of being done with convenience and with the
same ultimate result. To investigate this point,
suppose that $w =$ the whole amount of wages
which it is requisite to pay in building a house,
and that this does not alter when we vary,
within certain limits, the time employed in the
work, denoted by t. If the work goes on continuously, we shall, during each unit of time,
have an amount invested $= \dfrac{w}{t}$. The whole
amount of investment of capital will therefore
be represented by the area of a triangle whose
base is t and height w; that is, the investment
is $t \times \dfrac{w}{2}$. Thus when the whole expenditure
is ultimately the same, the amount of investment is simply proportional to the time. The
result would be more serious if compound interest during the time were taken into account;
but the consideration of compound or even
simple interest would render the formulæ very
complex, and is hardly requisite for the purposes I have in view.

We must clearly distinguish the case treated
above, in which the amount of labour is the
same, but spread over a longer time, from other
cases where the labour increases in proportion

to the time. The investment of capital, then, grows in an exceedingly rapid manner. Neglecting the first cost of tools, materials, and other preparations, let the first day's labour cost a; during the second day this remains invested, and the amount of capital a is added; on each following day a like addition is made. The amount of capital invested is evidently

At beginning of second day $\quad a,$

„ „ third „ $\quad a + a,$

„ „ fourth „ $\quad a + a + a;$

and so on. If the work lasts during $n + 1$ days, the total amount of investment of capital will be

$$a + 2a + 3a + 4a + \ldots \ldots n a.$$

The sum of the series is

$$a\left(\frac{n}{2} + \frac{n^2}{2}\right),$$

which increases by a term involving the square of the time. The employment of capital thus grows in proportion to the triangular numbers

$$1, \ 3, \ 6, \ 10, \ 15, \ 21, \ \&c.$$

If we regard the investment as taking place continuously, the whole absorption of capital is represented by the area of a right-angled triangle (Fig. XII), in which ob_1, $b_1 b_2$, $b_2 b_3$, &c. are the successive units of time. The heights

of the lines $a_1 b_1$, $a_2 b_2$ represent the amounts
invested at the ends of the times.   The daily

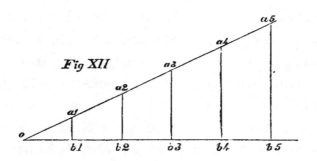

Fig XII

investment being a, the total amount of investment will be $a \dfrac{n^2}{2}$ increasing as the square
of the time.

Cases of this kind continually occur, as in
sinking a deep mine of which the requisite
depth cannot be previously known with accuracy.   Any large work, such as a breakwater,
an embankment, the foundations of a great
bridge, a dock, a long tunnel, the dredging of
a channel, involves a problem of a similar
nature; for it is seldom known what amount
of labour and capital will be required; and if
the work lasts much longer than is expected,
the result is usually a financial disaster.

Illustrations of the Investment of Capital.

The time during which capital remains invested, and the circumstances of its investment or reproduction, are exceedingly various in different employments. If a person plants cabbages, they will be ready in the course of a few months, and the labour of planting and tending them, together with a part of the labour of preparing and manuring the soil, yields its results with very little delay. In planting a forest tree, however, a certain amount of labour is expended, and no result obtained until the lapse of 30, 40, or 50 years. The first cost of enclosing, preparing, and planting a plantation is considerable ; and though, after a time, the loppings and thinnings of the trees repay the cost of superintendence and repairs, yet the absorption of capital is great, and we may thus account for the small amount of planting which goes on. The aging of wine is a somewhat similar case. A certain amount of labour is expended without result for 10 or 20 years. and the cost of storage is incurred during the whole time. To estimate the real cost of the articles at the end of the time, we must, in all such cases, add compound interest, and this grows in a rapid manner. For every pound invested at the commencement, the following is the growth by interest, at five per cent. per annum :

At commencement	. 1.00
At end of 10 years	1.63
20 ,, ...	2.65
30 ,, ...	4.32
40 ,, ...	7.04
50 ,, ...	11.47
60 ,, ...	18.68
70 ,, ...	30·43
80 ,, ...	49.56
90 ,, ...	80.73
100 ,, ...	131.50

If an annual charge, however small, has to be incurred (for instance, the cost of storage and superintendence), the cost mounts up in a still more alarming manner. Thus, if the cost is one pound per annum, the following are the amounts, with compound interest, invested after decennial intervals :

At the end of 10 years	12.58
20 ,, ...	33.07
30 ,, ...	66.44
40 ,, ...	120.80
50 ,, ...	209.35

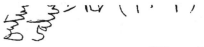

At the end of 60 years	353.58
70 ,, ...	588.53
80 ,, ...	971.23
90 ,, ...	1594.61
100 ,, ...	2610.03

An interesting example of the investment of capital occurs in the case of gold and silver, a large stock of which is maintained either in the form of money, or plate and jewellery. Labour is spent in the digging or mining of the metals, which is gradually repaid by the use or satisfaction arising from the possession of the metals during the whole time for which they continue in use. Hence the investment of capital extends over the average duration of the metals. Now, if the stock of gold requires one per cent. of its amount to maintain it undiminished, it will be apparent that each particle of gold remains in use 100 years on the average; if $\frac{1}{2}$ per cent is sufficient, the average duration will be 200 years. We may state the result thus :

Loss of gold or silver annually.		Average duration of each particle in use.
1 per cent.	.. ..	100 years
$\frac{1}{2}$,,	.. ..	200 ,,
$\frac{1}{4}$,,	.. ..	400 ,,
$\frac{1}{10}$,,	.. ..	1000 ,,

The wear and loss of the precious metals in a civilised country is probably not more than $\frac{1}{200}$ part annually, including plate, jewellery, and money in the estimate, so that the average investment will be for 200 years. It is curious that, if we regard a quantity of gold as wearing away annually by a fixed percentage of what remains, the duration of some part is infinite, and yet the average duration is finite. Some of the gold possessed by the Romans is doubtless mixed with what we now possess; and some small part of it will be handed down as long as the human race continues on the earth.

Fixed and Circulating Capital.

Economists have long been accustomed to distinguish capital into the two kinds, fixed and circulating. Adam Smith called that circulating which passes from hand to hand, and yields a revenue by being parted with. The fact of being frequently exchanged is, however, an accidental circumstance which leads to no results of importance. Ricardo altered the use of the terms, applying the name *circulating* to that which is frequently destroyed, and has to be reproduced. He says unequivocally [d]—' In proportion as fixed capital is less durable, it approaches to the nature of circulating capital. It will be consumed, and its value reproduced in a shorter time, in order to preserve the capital of the manufacturer.' Accepting this doctrine, and carrying it out to the full extent, we must say that no precise line can be drawn between the two kinds. The difference is one of amount and degree. The duration of capital may vary from a day to several hundred years; the most circulating is the least durable; the most fixed the most durable.

Free and Invested Capital.

I believe that the clear explanation of the doctrine of capital requires the use of a term *free capital*, which has not been hitherto recognised by economists. By free capital I mean the wages of labour, either in its transitory form of money, or its real form of food and other necessaries of life. The ordinary sustenance requisite to support labourers of all

[d] 'On the Principles of Political Economy and Taxation,' chap. i, § 5, third edition, p. 36.

ranks when engaged upon their work is really the true form of capital. It is quite in agreement with the ordinary language of commercial men not to say that a factory, or dock, or railway, or ship, *is capital,* but that *it represents so much capital sunk in the enterprise.* To invest capital is to spend money, or the food and maintenance which money purchases, upon the completion of some work. The capital remains invested or sunk until the work has returned profit, equivalent to the first cost, with interest. Much clearness would result from making the language of Economy more nearly coincident with that of commerce. Accordingly, I would not say that a railway *is fixed capital,* but that *capital is fixed in the railway.* The capital is not the railway, but the food of those who made the railway. Abundance of free capital in a country means that there are copious stocks of food, clothing, and every other article which people insist upon having; that, in short, everything is so arranged that abundant subsistence and conveniences of every kind are forthcoming without the labour of the country being much taxed to provide them. It is in such circumstances possible that a part of the labourers of the country can be employed in works of which the utility is distant, and yet no one will feel any scarcity in the present.

Uniformity of the Rate of Interest.

A most important principle of this subject is, that *free capital can be indifferently employed in any branch or kind of industry*. Free capital, as we have just seen, consists of a suitable assortment of all kinds of food, clothing, utensils, furniture, and other articles which a community requires for its ordinary sustenance. Men and families consume much the same kind of commodities, whatever may be the branch of manufacture or trade by which they earn a living. Hence there is nothing in the nature of free capital to determine its employment in one kind of industry rather than another. The very same wages, whether we regard the money wages, or the real wages purchased with the money, will support a man whether he be a mechanic, a weaver, a coal miner, a carpenter, a mason, or any other kind of labourer.

The necessary result is, that the rate of interest for free capital will tend to and closely attain uniformity in all employments. The market for capital is like all other markets : *there can be but one price for one article at one time.* Now the article in question is the same so that its price must be the same. Accordingly, the rate of interest, as is well known, when freed from considerations of risk, trouble, and other interfering causes, is the same in all trades; and every trade will employ capital up to the point at which it just yields the current interest. If any manufacturer or trader employs so much capital in supporting a certain amount of labour that the return is less than in other trades, he will lose; for he might have obtained the current rate by lending it to other traders.

General Expression for the Rate of Interest.

We may obtain a general expression for the rate of interest yielded by capital in any employment provided we may suppose that the produce varies for the same amount of labour, as some continuous function of the time elapsing between the expenditure of the labour and the enjoyment of the result. Let the time in question be t, and the produce for the same amount of labour ft, which may be supposed always to increase with t. If we now extend the time to $t + \triangle t$, the produce will be $f(t + \triangle t)$, and the increment of produce $f(t + \triangle t) - ft$. The ratio which this increment bears to the increment of investment of capital will determine the rate of interest. Now, at the end of the time t, we might receive the produce ft, and this is the amount of capital which remains invested when we extend the time by $\triangle t$. Hence the amount of increased investment of capital is $ft \cdot \triangle t$; and, dividing the increment of produce by this, we have

$$\frac{f(t + \triangle t) - ft}{\triangle t} \times \frac{1}{ft}.$$

When we reduce the magnitude of $\triangle t$ indefinitely, the limit of the first factor of the above is the differential coefficient of ft, so that we find the rate of interest to be represented by

$$\frac{d\,ft}{dt}\,\frac{1}{ft} \quad \text{or} \quad \frac{f't}{ft}.$$

The interest of capital is, in other words, the rate of increase of the produce divided by the whole produce; but this is a quantity which must rapidly approach to zero, unless means can be found of continually maintaining the rate of increase. Unless a body moves with a most rapidly increasing speed, the space it

moves over in any unit of time must ultimately become inconsiderable compared with
the whole space passed over from the commencement. There is no reason to suppose
that industry, generally speaking, is capable of
returning any such vastly increasing produce
from the greater application of capital. Every
new machine or other great invention will usually require a fixation of capital for a certain
average time, and may be capable of paying
interest upon it ; but when this average time
is reached, it fails to afford a return to more
prolonged investments.

To take an instance, let us suppose that the
produce of labour in some case is proportional
to the interval of abstinence t; then we have
say $ft = a \cdot t$. The differential coefficient $f't$ is
now a; and the rate of interest $\dfrac{a}{ft}$ or $\dfrac{a}{a\,t}$ or $\dfrac{1}{t}$;
or the rate of interest varies inversely as the
time of investment.

The Tendency of Profits to a Minimum.

It is one of the most favourite doctrines of
Political Economists from the time of Adam
Smith, that as society progresses and capital

accumulates, the rate of profit, or rather the
rate of interest, tends to fall. The rate will
always ultimately sink, so low, they think, that
the inducements to further accumulation will
cease.   This doctrine is in striking agreement
with the result of the somewhat abstract ana-
lytical investigation given above.   Our formula
for the rate of interest shows that unless there
be constant progress in the arts, the rate must
soon sink towards zero.   There are sufficient
statistical facts, too, to confirm the conclusion
historically.   The only question that can arise
is as to the actual cause of this tendency.

Adam Smith vaguely attributed it to the
competition of capitalists, saying, ' The increase
of stock which raises wages, tends to lower
profit.' When the stocks of many rich merchants are turned into the same trade, their
mutual competition naturally tends to lower
its profit ; and when there is a like increase of
stock in 'all the different trades carried on in
the same society, the same competition must
produce the same effect in all.'

Later economists have entertained different
views.   They attribute the fall of interest to
the rise in the cost of labour.   The produce of

labour, they say, is divided between capitalists and labourers, and if it is necessary to give more to labour, there must be less left to capital, and the rate of profit will fall. I shall discuss the validity of this theory in the final chapter, and will only here remark, that it is not in agreement with the view I have ventured to take of the origin of interest. I consider that interest is determined by the increment of produce which it enables labourers to obtain, and is altogether independent of the total return which he receives to this labour. In fact, the formula $\dfrac{f't}{ft}$ shows that the interest will be greater as the whole produce ft is less, if the advantage of more capital, measured by $f't$, remains unchanged. In many ill-governed countries, where the land is wretchedly tilled, the average produce is small, and yet the rate of interest is high, simply because the want of security prevents the due supply of capital : hence more capital is urgently needed, and its price is high. In America and the British Colonies the produce is often high, and yet interest is high, as there is not sufficient capital accumulated to meet all the demands. In England and other

old countries the rate of interest is generally
lower because there is an abundance of capital,
and the urgent need of more is not actually felt.

I conceive that the returns to capital and
labour are independent of each other. If the
soil yields little, and capital will not make it
yield more, then both wages and interest will
be low, if not attracted away to more profitable
employment. If the soil yields much, and capital will make it yield more, then both wages
and interest will be high; if the soil yields
much, and capital will not make it yield more,
then wages will be high and interest low,
unless the capital finds other investments. But
the subject is much complicated by the interference of rent. When we speak of the soil
yielding much, we must distinguish between
the *whole yield* and the *final rate of yield*. In
the Western States of America the land yields
a large total, and all at a high final rate, so
that the labourer enjoys the result. In England there is a large total yield, but a small
final yield, so that the landowner receives a
large rent and the labourer small wages. The
more fertile land having here been long in cultivation, the wages of the labourer are measured

by what he could earn out of the cultivation
of the sterile land which it only just pays to
take into cultivation.

The Advantage of Capital to Industry.

We must take great care not to confuse the
rate of interest on capital with the whole advantage which it confers on industry. The
rate of interest depends on the advantage of
the last increment of capital, and the advantages of previous increments may be greater in
almost any ratio. In considering the laws of
utility, we found that an article possessing an
indefinitely great total utility, for instance
corn or water, might have a low final degree
of utility, because our need of it was almost
satisfied ; yet the ratio of exchange always depends upon the final, not the previous utility.
The case is the same with capital. Some capital may be indispensable to a manufacture ;
hence the benefit conferred by the capital is
indefinitely great, and were there no more capital to be had, the rate of interest which could
be demanded would be almost unlimited. But
as soon as ever a larger supply of capital becomes available, the prior benefit of capital is

overlooked. As free capital is always the same in quality, the second portion may be made to replace the first if needful : hence capitalists can never exact from labourers the whole advantage which their capital confers—they can only exact a rate determined by the advantage of the last increment. A lender of capital cannot say to a borrower who wants £3,000—' I know that £1,000 is indispensable to your business, and therefore will charge you 100 per cent. interest upon it ; for the second £1,000, which is less necessary, I will charge 20 per cent. ; and as upon the third £1,000 you can only earn the common profit, I will only ask 5 per cent.' The answer would be, that there are many people only earning 5 per cent. on their capital who would be glad to lend at a small advance of interest ; and it is a matter of indifference who is the lender.

The general result of the uniformity of interest is, that the employers of capital always get it at the lowest prevailing rate ; they always borrow the capital which is least necessary to others, and either the labourers themselves, or the public generally as consumers, gather all the excess of advantage. To illustrate this, let distances along the line *ox*, in Fig. XIII, mark

quantities of capital employing in any branch
of industry a fixed number of labourers. Let
the area of the curve denote the whole produce
of labour and capital. Thus to the capital, *on*,
results a produce measured by the area of the
curvilinear figure between the upright lines *oy*
and *qn*. But the amount of increased produce

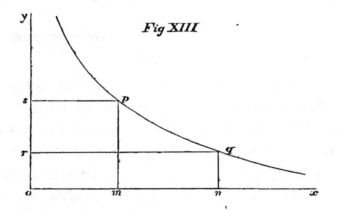

Fig XIII

which would be due to an increment of capital
would be measured by the line *qn*, so that this
will be *f′t*. The whole interest of the capital
will be its amount, *on*, multiplied by the rate
qn, or the area of the rectangle *oq*. The re-
mainder of the produce, *pqry*, will belong to
the labourer. But had less capital been available, say not more than *om*, its rate of interest
would have been measured by *pm*, the amount
of interest by the rectangle *op*, while the

labourer must have remained contented with the smaller share, *psy*. I will not say that the above diagram represents with strict accuracy the relations of capital, produce, wages, rate of interest, and amount of interest ; but it may serve roughly to illustrate their relations. I see no way of exactly representing the theory of capital in the form of a diagram.

Are Articles in the Consumers' hands Capital?

The views of the nature of capital expressed in this chapter generally agree with those entertained by Ricardo and various other economists ; but there is one point in which the theory leads me to a result at variance with the opinions of almost all writers. I feel quite unable to adopt the opinion that the moment goods pass into the possession of the consumer they cease altogether to have the attributes of capital. This doctrine descends to us from the time of Adam Smith, and has generally received the undoubting assent of his followers. The latter, indeed, have generally omitted all notice of such goods, treating them as if no longer under the view of the economist. Adam Smith, although he denied the possessions of a consumer the name of capital, took care to enumerate them as part of the *stock* of the community. He divides into three portions the general stock of a country, and while the second and third portions are fixed and circulating capital, the first is described as follows [e]—

'The first is that portion which is reserved for immediate consumption, and of which the characteristic is, that it affords no revenue or profit. It consists in the stock of food, clothes, household furniture, &c., which have been purchased by their proper consumers, but which are not yet entirely consumed. The whole stock of mere dwelling-houses, too, subsisting at any one time in the country, make a part of this first portion. The stock that is laid out in a house, if it is to be the dwelling-house of the proprietor, ceases from that moment to serve in the function of a capital, or to afford any revenue to its owner. A dwelling-house, as such, contributes nothing to the revenue of its inhabitant; and though it is, no doubt, extremely useful to him, it is as his clothes and household furniture are useful to him, which, however, make a part of his expense, and not of his revenue.'

[e] 'Wealth of Nations,' book ii. chap. 1.

Mr. MacCulloch, indeed, in his edition of the 'Wealth of Nations' (p. 121), has remarked upon this passage, that 'The capital laid out in building houses for such persons is employed as much for the public advantage as if it were vested in the tools or instruments they make use of in their respective businesses.' He appears, in fact, to reject the doctrine, and it is surprising that economists have generally acquiesced in Adam Smith's view, though it leads to manifest contradictions. It leads to the absurd conclusion, that the very same thing fulfilling the very same purposes will be capital or not according to its accidental ownership. To procure good port wine, it is necessary to keep it for a number of years, and Adam Smith would not deny that a stock of wine kept in the wine merchant's possession for this purpose is capital, because it yields him revenue. If a consumer buys it when new, and keeps it to improve, it will not be capital, although it is evident that he gains the same profit as the merchant by buying it at a lower price. If a coal merchant lays in a stock of coal when cheap, to sell when dear, it is capital; but if a consumer lays in a stock, it is not.

Adam Smith's views seem to be founded upon

a notion, that capital ought to give an annual revenue or increase of wealth like a field yields a crop of corn or grass.   Speaking of a dwelling-house, he says: 'If it is to be let to a tenant for rent, as the house itself can produce nothing, the tenant must always pay the rent out of some other revenue, which he derives either from labour, or stock, or land. Though a house, therefore, may yield a revenue to its proprietor, and thereby serve in the function of a capital to him, it cannot yield any to the public, nor serve in the function of a capital to it, and the revenue of the whole body of the people can never be in the smallest degree increased by it.   Clothes and household furniture, in the same manner, sometimes yield a revenue, and thereby serve in the function of a capital to particular persons.   In countries where masquerades are common, it is a trade to let out masquerade dresses for a night.   Upholsterers frequently let furniture by the month or by the year.   Undertakers let the furniture of funerals by the day and by the week.   Many people let furnished houses and get a rent, not only for the use of the house, but for that of the furniture.   The revenue, however, which is derived from such things, must always be ultimately drawn from some other source of revenue.'

This notion that people live upon a kind of net revenue flowing in to them appears to be derived from the old French economists, and plays no part in modern Political Economy. Nothing is more requisite than a dwelling-house, and if a person cannot hire a house at the required spot, he must find capital to build it. I think that no economist would refuse to count among the fixed capital of the country that which is sunk in dwelling-houses. Capital is sunk in farming that we may have bread, in cotton-mills that we may be clothed, and why not in houses that we may be lodged? If land yields an annual revenue of corn and wool, milk, beef, and other necessaries, houses yield a revenue of shelter and comfort. The sole end of all industry is to satisfy our wants; and if capital is requisite to supply shelter, and furniture and useful utensils, as it undoubtedly is, why refuse it the name which it bears in all other employments?

Can we deny that the property of a hotel-keeper is capital and yields a revenue to its owner? Yet it is invested in pots and pans, and beds, and all kinds of common furniture.

In America it is not uncommon for people to live all their lives in hotels or boarding-houses; and we might readily conceive the system to advance until no one undertook housekeeping except as a profession.   Now if we allow to what is invested in hotels the nature of capital, I do not see how we can refuse it to common houses.   We should thus be led into all kinds of absurdities.   For instance, if two people live in their own houses, these are not, according to present opinion, capital; if they find it convenient to exchange houses and pay rent each to the other, the houses are capital.   It is a regular trade in watering places to furnish houses and let them : surely it is capital which is embarked in the trade.   If a private individual happens to own a furnished house which he does not at the time want, and lets it, can we refuse to regard his house and furniture as capital ?   Whenever one person provides the articles and another uses them and pays rent, there is capital.   Surely, then, if the same person uses and owns them, the nature of the things is not fundamentally different.   There is no need for a money payment to pass; but every person who keeps accurate accounts should debit those accounts with an annual charge for interest and depreciation on what he has invested in house and furniture. Housekeeping is an occupation involving wages, capital and interest, like any other business, except that the owner consumes the whole result.

By accepting this view of the subject, we shall avoid endless difficulties. What, for instance, shall we say to a theatre? Is it not the product of capital? Can it be erected without capital? Does it not return interest, if successful, like any cotton mill, or steam vessel? If the economist agrees to this, he must allow, on similar grounds, that a very large part of the aggregate capital of the country is invested in theatres, hotels, schools, lecture rooms, and institutions of various kinds which do not belong to the industry of the country, taken in a narrow sense, but which none the less contribute to the wants of its inhabitants, which is the sole object of all industry.

I may add, that even the food, clothes, and many other possessions of extensive classes are often capital because they are bought upon credit, and interest is undoubtedly paid for the capital sunk in them by the dealers. There is hardly, I suppose, a man of fashion in London who walks in his own clothes, and the tailors find in the practice a very profitable investment for capital. Except among the poorer classes, and often among them, food is never paid for until some time after it is consumed. Interest must be paid one way or another upon the capital thus absorbed.

Whether or not these articles in the consumers' hands are *capital,* at any rate they have capital invested in them—that is, labour has been spent upon them of which the whole benefit is not enjoyed at once.

I might also point out at almost indefinite length, that the stock of food, clothing, and other requisite articles of subsistence in the country are what compose a main element of capital according to the statements of Mr. Mill, Professor Fawcett, and most other economists. Now what does it really matter if these articles happen to lie in the warehouses of traders or in private houses, so long as there is a stock? At present it is the practice for farmers or corn merchants to hold the produce of the harvest until the public buys and consumes it. Surely the stock of corn is capital? But if it were the practice of every housekeeper to buy up corn in the autumn and keep it in a private granary, would it not serve in exactly the same way to subsist the population? Would not everything go on exactly the same, except that every one would be his own capitalist in regard to corn in place of paying farmers and corn merchants for doing the business?

CHAPTER VIII.

CONCLUDING REMARKS.

The Doctrine of Population.

IT is no part of my object in this work to attempt to trace out, with any approach to completeness, the results of the theory given in the preceding chapters. When the views of the nature of Value, and the general method of treating the subject by the application of the fluxional calculus, have received some recognition and acceptance, it will be time enough to think of results. I shall only further occupy a few pages in pointing out the branches of economical doctrine which have been omitted, and indicating their connection with the theory.

The doctrine of population has been conspicuously absent, not because I in the least doubt its truth and vast importance, but because it forms no part of the direct problem of Economy. I do not at the moment remember to have seen it remarked by any writer, that it is a total inversion of the problem to treat labour as a varying quantity, when we originally start with labour as the first element of production, and aim at the most economical employment of that labour. The great problem of Economy may, as it seems to me, be stated thus :—*Given, a certain population, with various needs and powers of production, in possession of certain lands and other sources of material : required, the mode of employing their labour so as to maximise the utility of the produce.* It is what mathematicians would call a change of the variable, afterwards to treat that labour, which is first a fixed quantity, as variable. It really amounts to altering the conditions of the problem so as to create at each variation a new problem. The same results, too, would generally be obtained by supposing the other conditions to vary. Given, a certain population, we may imagine the land and capital at their disposal to be greater or less, and may then trace out the results which will, in most respects, be applicable to a less or greater population with the original land and capital.

The Relation of Wages and Profit.

There is another inversion of the problem of
Economy which is generally made in works
upon the subject. Although labour is the starting-point in production, and the interests of the
labourers the very object of the science, yet
economists do not progress far before they
suddenly turn round and treat labour as a
commodity which is bought up by capitalists.
Labour becomes itself the object of the laws of
supply and demand, instead of those laws act-
ing in the distribution of the products of labour.
Political Economists have invented, too, a very
simple theory to determine the rate of wages
at which capital can buy up labour. The average rate of wages, they say, is found by dividing
the whole amount of capital appropriated to the
payment of wages by the number of the labourers paid ; and they wish us to believe that this
settles the question. But a very little consideration will show that this proposition is simply
a *truism*. The average rate of wages must be
equal to what is appropriated to the purpose
divided by the number who share it. The whole
question will consist in determining how much
is appropriated for the purpose; for it certainly

need not be the whole existing amount of circulating capital. Mr. Mill distinctly says, that because industry is limited by capital, we are not to infer that it always reaches that limit[a]; and, as a matter of fact, we often observe that there is abundance of capital to be had at low rates of interest, while there are also large numbers of artisans starving for want of employment. The wage-fund theory is therefore wholly illusory as a real solution of the problem, though I do not deny that it may have a certain limited and truthful application, to be shortly considered.

Another part of the current doctrines of Economy determines the rate of profit of capitalists in a very simple manner. The whole product of industry must be divided into the portions paid as rent, taxes, profits, and wages. We may exclude taxes as exceptional, and not very important. Rent also may be eliminated, for it is essentially variable, and is reduced to zero in the case of the poorest land cultivated. We thus arrive at the simple equation—

$$\text{Produce} = \text{profit} + \text{wages}.$$

A very simple result also is drawn from the

[a] 'Principles of Political Economy,' book i. chap. 5, § 2.

S

formula ; for we are told that if wages rise, profits must fall, and *vice versâ*. But such a doctrine is radically fallacious ; *it involves the attempt to determine two unkown quantities from one equation.* I grant that if the produce be a fixed amount, then if wages rise profits must fall, and *vice versâ*. Something might perhaps be made of this doctrine if Ricardo's theory of a natural rate of wages, that which is just sufficient to support the labourer, held true. But I altogether question the existence of any such rate. The wages of working men in this kingdom vary from perhaps ten shillings a week up to forty shillings or more, the minimum in one part of the country is not the minimum in another. It is utterly impossible, too, to define exactly what are the necessaries of life. I am inclined, therefore, altogether to reject the current doctrines as to the rate of wages ; and even if the theory held true of any one class of labourers, there is the additional difficulty that we have to account for the very different rates which prevail in different trades. It is quite impossible that we should accept for ever Ricardo's sweeping simplification of the subject involved in the assumption, that there is a natural ordinary rate of wages for common labour, and that all higher rates are merely exceptional instances, to be explained away on other grounds.

The view which I should hold of the rate of wages is not more difficult to comprehend than the current one. It is, that the wages of a working man are ultimately coincident with what he produces, after the deduction of rent, taxes, and the interest of capital. I think that in the equation

$$\text{Produce} = \text{profit} + \text{wages},$$

the quantity of produce is essentially variable, and that profit is the part to be first determined. If we resolve profit into wages of superintendence, insurance against risk, and interest, the first part is really wages itself; the second equalises the result in different employments; and the interest is, I believe, determined as stated in the last chapter.

The reader will observe the important qualification, that wages are only *ultimately* thus determined—that is, in the long run, and on the average of any one branch of employment.

The fact that workmen are not their own capitalists introduces complexity into the problem. The capitalists, or *entrepreneurs*, enter as a distinct interest. It is they who project

and manage a branch of production, and form
estimates as to the expected produce.   It is
the amount of this produce which incites them
to invest capital and buy up labour.   They pay
the lowest current rates for the kind of labour
required ; and if the produce exceeds the average, those who are first in the field make large
profits.   This soon induces competition on the
part of other capitalists, who, in trying to obtain
good workmen, will raise the rate of wages.
This competition will proceed until the point is
reached at which only the regular market rate
of interest is obtained for the capital invested.
At the same time wages will have been so
raised, that the workmen reap the whole excess
of produce, unless indeed the price of the produce has fallen, and the public, as consumers,
have the benefit.   Whether this latter result
will follow or not, depends upon the number
of labourers who are fitted for the work.   Where
much skill and education is required, extensive
competition will be impossible, and a perma-
nently high rate of wages will exist.   But if
only common labour is requisite, the price of
the goods cannot be maintained, wages will fall
to their former point, and the public have the
advantage of cheaper supplies.

It will be observed, that this account of the matter involves the temporary application of the wage-fund theory. It is the proper function of capitalists to sustain labour before the result is accomplished, and as many branches of industry require a large outlay long previous to any definitive result being arrived at, it follows that capitalists must undertake the risk of any branch of industry where the ultimate profits are not accurately known. But we now have some clue as to the amount of capital which will be appropriated to the payment of wages in any trade. The amount of capital will depend on the amount of anticipated profits, and the competition to obtain proper workmen will strongly tend to secure to the latter all their legitimate share in the ultimate produce. For instance, let a number of schemes be set on foot for laying telegraphic cables. The ultimate profits are very uncertain, depending upon the utility of the cables as compared with their cost. If capitalists make a large estimate of those profits, they will apply much capital to the immediate manufacture of the cables. All workmen competent at the moment to be employed will be hired, and high wages paid if necessary. Every man who has peculiar skill,

knowledge, or experience, rendering his assistance valuable, will be hired at any requisite
cost.   At this point it is the wage-fund theory
that is in operation.   But, after a certain number of years, the condition of affairs will be
totally different.   Capitalists will learn, by experience, exactly what the profits of cables may
be; that amount of capital will be thrown into
the work which finds the average amount of
profits, and neither more nor less.   The cost of
transmitting messages will be reduced by competition, so that no excessive profits are made
by any of the parties concerned; the rate of
wages, therefore, of every species of labour will
be reduced to the average proper to labour of
that degree of skill.   But if there be required
in any branch of the work a very special kind
of skilled and experienced labour, it will not
be affected by competition in the same way,
and the wages or salary will remain high.

I think that it is in this way quite possible
to reconcile theories which are at first sight
so different.   The wage-fund theory acts in
a wholly temporary manner.   Every labourer
ultimately receives the due value of his produce after paying a proper fraction to the
capitalist.   At the same time workers of dif-

ferent degrees of skill, receive very different shares according as they contribute a common or a scarce kind of labour to the result.

Professor Hearn's Views.

I have the more pleasure and confidence in putting forward these somewhat heretical views concerning the general problem of Economy, inasmuch as they are nearly identical with those arrived at by Professor Hearn, of Melbourne University. It would be a somewhat long task to trace out exactly the coincidence of opinions between us, but he certainly adopts the notion that the capitalist merely buys up temporarily the prospects of the concern he manages and the labourers he employs. Thus he says—' In place of having a share in the undertaking, the co-operator sells for a stipulated price his labour or the use of his capital. The case therefore comes within the ordinary conditions of exchange ; and the price of labour and the price of capital are determined in the same manner as all other questions of price are determined. Yet the general character of the partnership is not destroyed. Although each particular transaction amounts to a sale, yet for the continuance of the business a nearer

connection arises.   Although the whole loss of
the undertaking, if the undertaking be unfortunate, falls upon the last proprietor, and the
interests of the other parties have been previously secured, yet each such loss prevents a
repetition of the transaction from which it
arose.   The capital which ought to have been
replaced, and which, if replaced, would have
afforded the means of employing labour and of
defraying the interest upon other capital, has
disappeared; and thus the market for labour
and for capital is by so much diminished.   Both
the labourer and the intermediate capitalist are
therefore directly concerned in the success of
every enterprise towards which they have con-
tributed.   If it be successful, they feel the advantage ; if it be not successful, they feel in
like manner the loss.   But this community of
interest is no longer direct, but is indirect
merely; and it arises not from the gains or the
losses of partners, but from the increased utility,
or the diminished demands of customers.'

   This passage really contains a statement of
the views which I am inclined wholly to accept; but no passages which I can select will
convey a true notion of the enlightened view
which Professor Hearn takes of the industrial

structure of society in his admirable work, 'Plutology.'[b] I know not what accidental circumstance, the distant residence of the author, or the unfortunate selection of a title, for instance, has diverted attention from the singular excellence and independence of his work.

The Noxious Influence of Authority.

I have but a few lines more to add. I have ventured in the preceding pages to call in question not a few of the favourite doctrines of economists. To me it is far more pleasant to agree than to differ ; but it is impossible that he who has any regard for truth can long avoid protesting against doctrines which seem to him erroneous. There is ever a tendency of a most hurtful kind to allow opinions to crystallise into creeds. Especially does this tendency manifest itself when some eminent author, with the power of clear and comprehensive exposition, becomes recognised as an authority on the subject. His works may possibly be far the best which are extant ; they may combine more truth with less error than we can elsewhere find. But any man must err, and the best

b Macmillan and Co., London.

T

works should ever be open to criticism. If, instead of welcoming inquiry and criticism, the admirers of a great author accept his writings as authoritative, both in their excellences and defects, the most serious injury is done to truth. In matters of philosophy and science authority has ever been the great opponent of truth. A despotic calm is the triumph of error ; in the republic of the sciences sedition and even anarchy are commendable.

In the physical sciences authority has greatly lost its noxious influence. Chemistry, in its brief existence of a century, has undergone three or four complete revolutions of theory. In the science of light, Newton's own authority has been decisively set aside, after it had retarded for nearly a century the progress of inquiry. Astronomers have not hesitated, within the last few years, to alter their estimate of all the dimensions of the planetary system and the universe, because good reasons had been shown for calling in question the real coincidence of previous measurements. In science and philosophy nothing must be held sacred. Truth itself is indeed sacred, but where is the absolute criterion of truth ?

I have added these words because I think

there is some fear of the too great influence of authoritative writers in Political Economy. I protest against deference for any man being allowed to check inquiry. Our science is becoming far too much a stagnant one, in which opinions rather than experience and reason are appealed to.

There are valuable suggestions towards the improvement of the science contained in the works of such writers as Senior, Banfield, Cairnes, Jennings, and Hearn, not to mention such original foreign authors as Courcelle-Seneuil or Bastiat ; but they are neglected because they do not happen to have been adopted in more widely-studied works. Under these circumstances it is a positive service to break the monotonous repetition of current questionable doctrines, even at the risk of new error. I trust that the theory now given may prove accurate; but, however this may be, it will not be useless if it cause inquiry to be directed into the true basis and form of a science which touches so directly the material welfare of the human race.

FINIS.

O

6.

CPSIA information can be obtained
at www.ICGtesting.com
Printed in the USA
BVHW040808130619
550809BV00022B/100/P